The Coaching Advantage

Move Forward

Lead Confidently

Accelerate Performance

MARCEL SANCHEZ

Move Forward   Lead Confidently   Accelerate Performance

This book is NOT for people that have "arrived" at their destination in life and **simply want to coast stress-free for the next thirty years.**

This book is for *courageous* senior executives, business leaders, entrepreneurs, and small business owners ready to maximize their education, amplify their skills, leverage their experiences, and build stronger relationships to move their lives forward and realize the greater impact.

These self-starting leaders endeavor to learn continuously. They give their very best to love their families better, influence their employees, challenge their colleagues, grow their clients, and revitalize their communities.

Is this daring book for *you*?

If your answer is yes, let's get moving!

The Coaching Advantage

© 2023 by Marcel Sanchez

Printed in the United States of America

Publisher: Amazon KDP Select

ISBN: 9798387546365

Cover designed by Savanah Sanchez
www.SavanahSanchez.com

Unless otherwise indicated, all Scripture quotations are from The Holy Bible, English Standard Version® (ESV®), copyright © 2001 by Crossway, a publishing ministry of Good News Publishers. Used by permission. All rights reserved.

No part of the book may be reproduced in any form without written permission of Marcel Sanchez, except in the case of brief quotations within critical articles and reviews.

Marcel Sanchez

Certified Professional Coach
Founder, Imagine Coaching Academy
17701 NW 57th Avenue
Miami, FL 33055
Direct: 786-554-0312
www.ImagineCoachingAcademy.com

Table of Contents

1. Remove Your Blind Spots — 11
Let Others Show You What You Can't See

2. Shift Your Mindset — 27
Replace Disempowering Fears with Empowering Confidence

3. Get Yourself Out Of The Way — 41
Accelerate Your Performance From Good to Great

4. Don't Sabotage Your Marriage — 57
Intentionally Direct, Protect, and Grow Your Marriage

5. Be Present and Engaged With Your Children — 87
Personally Love, Encourage, and Train Your Children

6. Stop Being Lazy and Start Moving Forward — 105
Leverage Discipline to Advance Through Your Obstacles

7. Clarify, Evoke, Align, and Focus — 133
Create an Intentional Life Plan to Maximize Your Impact

8. Stop Dreaming and Get to Work — 161
Start Your Next Visionary Adventure With One Step

9. Get Better Faster — 179
Increase Your Performance With Hybrid Coaching and Training

10. Look Up — 201
Discover Your Life's Purpose Outside of Yourself

Conclusion: Your Coaching Advantage — 237

Introduction

Welcome to *The Coaching Advantage* and this new adventure. After many years of professional training, consulting, and coaching, I discovered a consistent theme among several highly successful business leaders.

These top performers were responsible for managing hundreds—and sometimes thousands—of employees. They consistently directed millions of dollars in monthly recurring revenue. Operationally speaking, they managed some of the most complex systems in today's modern world.

Although these high-capacity leaders were some of the most respected top influencers in their industry, they all had one common undercurrent that ignited their passion and sustained their performance. I've narrowed this consistent theme down to one simple phrase.

Get Better Faster

This was the common denominator among them. Each one of these high-impact leaders had a relentless pursuit of achieving excellence in every area of their lives, including their business,

They wanted to accelerate their skills along with their performance at work. These leaders were determined to stay ahead of their competitors and empower their people to serve their clients better than they ever could've expected or imagined.

They wanted to spend more time—both in quantity and quality—with their family and friends. They were determined to build their marriage and coach their children to thrive at school and excel in life. These leaders were deeply committed to their families. They wanted to make the most of every moment with the people they loved to spend time with every day.

These self-starting leaders looked for practical ways to assist their communities. They wanted to serve their churches and fund local community centers and nonprofits. At times their dreams were so big that they overwhelmed them, but only for a minute.

One of the things that impressed me the most was their desire for *total alignment*. They wanted to align every area of their lives with their core values. They hadn't arrived yet, but they were hyper-focused on getting there as soon as possible.

Do you love a good challenge?

I know that you do. If it weren't the case, you would've stopped reading by now. This book is designed to challenge you to become increasingly more vulnerable and transparent about the things you often think about and envision but seldom verbalize. We all have these recurring thoughts.

It's a personal challenge from me to you. Like these amazing leaders we've mentioned, I consider you to be among the top leaders in your industry. Every challenge requires a commitment. But you already knew that, right?

Move Forward   Lead Confidently   Accelerate Performance

How can you get the most out of this book?

To get the most out of this book, I'm going to ask you to *commit* to the following action steps.

1. After reading through the introduction, divide your reading time into **ten sessions** over the next **ten days**.

2. Read only **one chapter** per session. The chapters are relatively short. This is intentional.

3. **Thoughtfully** answer each question presented within the contents of each chapter.

4. At the end of each session, read the questions from the **Questions for Reflection** section. Write down your responses in the space provided.

5. **Separate 20-30 minutes to reflect** deeper on key chapter points and your responses to each question.

You will get the *most* out of this book—and better understand what areas of your life need more focus, energy, and direction—as you commit to working through these essential action steps.

Enjoy your journey!

Coach Marcel

The International Coaching Federation (ICF) defines coaching as

"partnering with clients in a thought-provoking and creative process that inspires them to maximize their personal and professional potential.

The process of coaching often unlocks previously untapped sources of imagination, productivity, and leadership."[1]

---

[1] "What is Coaching?" International Coaching Federation, ICF.org, December 21, 2021, https://coachingfederation.org/about

Chapter 1

Remove Your Blind Spots

Let Others Show You What You Can't See

Exposing Coaching Myths

Myth #1 – Today, the only effective form of coaching is in-person coaching.

The Real Story

The effectiveness of coaching is not measured exclusively by the form of coaching but rather by the effectiveness in helping you move forward along your journey. Coaching over phone calls and video meetings has proved to be a highly effective modality.

We're often left mesmerized by their staggering performance. Against all odds—and with only a few seconds on the clock—these professional athletes repeatedly find jaw-dropping ways to lead their team to another amazing victory.

Exceptional seems to fall short of their freakish talent. And best of all, they perform their skills before enormous crowds with artistic beauty and managed grace. Are they really aliens cleverly disguised as humans from outer space?

Maybe, or maybe not.

These elite athletes make it look so easy and painless, but we all know better. It requires an uncommon level of commitment, energy, and focus to compete at their level *consistently* each week.

What often surprises most of us is the fact that many—if not all—of these athletes hire professional coaches to get better faster. Are you serious?

These men and women are at the top of their game. They break records with great ease. They're in the best shape of their lives. Some of them earn over $500,000 per game. Why in the world would they need anyone to coach them? They should start coaching others, right?

Wrong!

Here's the reality you and I often forget. All of us have blind spots. We all have areas in our lives that are not performing at 100% capacity every day. You have them, I have them, and these elite athletes have them too.

The issue is not that you don't want to perform at your very best. I have no doubt that you most certainly want to be at the top of your game.

Who wouldn't be, right?

The problem—and the large elephant in the room—is that you *can't* see the cracks in your life that others see with great clarity and objectivity.

You can't see the shift in your approach, the change in attitude, the slide in your behavior, or the limiting beliefs in your thinking.

All of us have blind spots. We all have areas in our lives that are not performing at 100% capacity every day.

You can't hear the forcefulness in your tone, the discouraging indifference in your responses, or the abrupt disruptions you regularly provoke in the lives of those around you.

What makes matters worse is that your past performance—in business, education, investing, or competitions—often *blinds* you to your present reality.

The issue is NOT that you don't want to perform at your very best. I have no doubt that you most certainly want to be at the top of your game. Who wouldn't be, right?

The problem—and the large elephant in the room—is that you can't see the cracks in your life that others see with great clarity and objectivity.

Blind spots stop progress

Do you want to get more out of life, but for some reason, the more part regularly escapes your grip?

Jeremy (not his real name) was educated, ambitious, socially adept, and experienced in his industry. He was highly respected by his peers, sought after by his clients, and celebrated among his friends and neighbors.

It seemed that Jeremy had all that life could offer him and more. But Jeremy wanted so much more in life.

Jeremy's life suddenly shifted in 2022. He was met with an unexpected lawsuit, a deterioration in his family life, a devastating theft in his business, and increasing debt to make matters even worse.

There was an ever-increasing crack in Jeremy's life—a blind spot that Jeremy could not see.

Do you want to get more out of life, but for some reason, the more part regularly escapes your grip?

Honestly, Jeremy didn't want to see it. When the subject was introduced, it was quickly deflected without an honest consideration of the facts.

Jeremy continued to plow ahead, expanding his hours at work, adding more appointments on the calendar, and trying to please everyone. Watching his desire for more repeatedly fall flat was difficult.

Many self-help resources, productivity books, business articles, and industry blogs say that removing blind spots in personal performance can lead to an average improvement of 15-25% in overall performance.

What would that increase do for your business?

How would that impact your family?

How would that change better serve your clients?

What else would change because of this increase?

Amazingly, and for several months, Jeremy managed to maintain a positive attitude throughout all the pressures and challenges he experienced. Unfortunately, he never permitted anyone to enter the struggle to explore what he was truly facing on the inside—at the soul level.

Jeremy's default was to continue working long hours to push things forward. He was very guarded about how he felt as he worked through some of the greatest difficulties in his life.

What got you here won't get you there.

Jeremy's motivational "let's get it done" attitude was inspirational to those around him, but it was also highly insufficient for what he needed. What got Jeremy to the success he experienced in life was not enough to get him to where he wanted to be next. The same principle applies to your life too.

What got you *here* won't get you *there*. What got you to the level of sustainable success that you're experiencing today is totally *insufficient* to get you to the next level of success you want to achieve tomorrow.

For Jeremy—and you and so many others—working longer hours is never the answer to get to the next level in life. Moreover, it serves to work against everything you desire to do.

Unlike Jeremy, your blind spots don't have to remain ignored and unexplored. You won't improve them if you continue to ignore them.

What got you here won't get you there.

What got you to the level of sustainable success that you're experiencing today is totally insufficient to get you to the next level of success you want to achieve tomorrow.

Revelation is powerful

Think for a minute about the way you approach life today. Consider life's finest gifts: faith, marriage, children, family, church, health, friends, work, neighbors, education, and vacations.

Are you plowing through these areas in your life because that's what you've always done in the past?

Are you cranking up the weekly hours at work at the expense of your family? Is your current pace of life *sustainable* over the long term?

Have you sacrificed your faith on the altar of materialism, travel, apathy, or isolation?

What blind spots can't you see clearly today? Well, you really don't know until someone tells you the truth. The reason is simple. You are blind to these spots in your life.

And the more comfortable you get with living with these blind spots, the less impactful work you will do. And in the process, the people you know and love will be affected in one way or another.

The questions must be raised, "What is a blind spot?" and "How do you remove your blind spots?" to gain clarity on what to do and what not to do.

The dictionary defines a blind spot as a portion of a field that cannot be seen or inspected with available equipment, an area in which one fails to exercise judgment or discrimination.[2]

---

[2] Merriam-Webster.com Dictionary, s.v. "blind spot," accessed January 2, 2023, https://www.merriam-webster.com/dictionary/blind%20spot

"The first step in removing blind spots is to acknowledge that they exist.

Once you accept that you have blind spots, you can start to actively work on identifying them and taking steps to address them."[3]

---

[3] "How to Identify and Remove Blind Spots in Your Business." Forbes, 24 Jan. 2023, www.forbes.com/sites/forbesbusinesscouncil/2019/01/12/how-to-identify-and-remove-blind-spots-in-your-business/?sh=6a54a16d7599

A *blind spot* in our context is a specific area of your character or performance that you can't see, but its direct impact on your life is obvious. It is most certainly an area of personal weakness. It debilitates the rest of your character, your performance, or both when ignored or denied.

The second question, "How do you remove your blind spots?" is a trick question. You can't remove your blind spots because you can't see them.

To remove the blind spots in your life, you need to allow someone else to identify what they are, define each one, and lead you through a process of discovery, self-awareness, and removal.

Someone else must help you *identify* your blind spots, *define* each blind spot, and lead you through a process to *remove* these blind spots as you gain increasing clarity one step at a time. Remember, you must let others show you what you can't see.

Let's review. To remove the blind spots in your life, you need to allow someone else to identify what they are, define each one, and lead you through a process of discovery, self-awareness, and removal.

This may seem like a ton of work, but in all truthfulness, it's good work that yields much fruit. And who do you know that doesn't enjoy the taste of much fruit, especially when it is fresh?

A blind spot in our context is a specific area of your character or performance that you can't see, but its direct impact on your life is obvious. It is most certainly an area of personal weakness.

When ignored or denied, it serves to debilitate the rest of your character, or your performance, or both.

The Coaching Advantage

Advantage #1

"Executive coaching is one of the key strategies recommended to support leaders as they shape and manage their organization's culture.

Executive coaching can help leaders develop the skills and mindset needed to create a healthy and productive workplace culture."[4]

---

[4] Gregersen, H. B., & Van Oosten, E. B. (2018). The Leader's Guide to Corporate Culture: How to Manage the Eight Critical Elements of Organizational Life. John Wiley & Sons.

Karen's Coaching Advantage

She was one of the most creative and passionate women I had ever met. Karen's energy flowed through her charismatic charm. She was inspirational and forward-thinking, aggressive, and yet uniquely humble.

Karen—like all of us—had significant blind spots to identify, explore, and overcome. You would think that this high-performing executive was totally unstoppable. After all, she overflowed with increasing confidence and optimism.

But on the inside, everything was different. The person on the outside did not match the one on the inside. Karen was conflicted internally. She was unable to identify the real issue holding her back.

As we worked through several inconsistencies in Karen's behavior and got to the root cause of her procrastination, Karen took a deep breath and took her next step forward.

Until we began meeting, Karen was caught in a debilitating cycle of doubt—her blind spot. She had allowed her past to keep her in a mental prison without having the key to open the door.

When Karen and I walked through this process together, she was the one who identified her blind spot, the source of this reality, the impact of her decisions, and what she needed to do to move her life forward with greater emotional and relational congruency.

What gave Karen the Coaching Advantage? She was willing to stop making excuses and start taking responsibility for where she wanted to go in life.

Move Forward   Lead Confidently   Accelerate Performance

Questions for Reflection

1. What blind spots have others pointed out in your character as it relates to your spouse, your children, your family, or your work?

2. Recently, what blind spots have you been ignoring or denying?

3. Is your tendency to continue plowing ahead to get things done or to stop and reflect deeply along the way?

4. What was the most powerful and humbling revelation someone ever gave you about your character?

5. How did you respond to their observation?

6. What benefits have you experienced by having a trusted person tell you the truth about your performance at work, in your marriage, with your family, at church, or with your health?

7. What action step can you start right away to give you a new advantage related to your blind spots?

Chapter 2

Shift Your Mindset

Replace Disempowering Fears With Empowering Confidence

Mindset is a *fixed* pattern of thinking. It's a combination of attitude, posture, and approach. By itself, your mindset is neutral. It can be used to remove energy and focus from your productivity or infuse electricity and enthusiasm into your work.

Your mindset will serve to maximize your time, or it will serve to waste your time.

Mindset is a fixed pattern of thinking.

Your mindset will act as the catalyst to move your business forward and take calculated risks or act as the decelerator and plateau your business.

Your mindset will lead you to train and develop your employees in the same way it worked 25 years ago or leverage effective technologies and soft skills training to empower them today.

Your mindset will keep you working long hours while sacrificing your spouse and children on the altar of getting ahead, or it will force you to cheat on your work to spend generous quality time with your family.

Your mindset will keep you believing that certain obstacles can't ever be overcome, or it will challenge you to face them head-on and get to their root cause faster.

Exposing Coaching Myths

Myth #2 – Coaching may motivate you temporarily, but it can't provide practical help to make a real difference in your life.

The Real Story

Professional coaching provides you with greater clarity, alignment, focus, and action. **It helps move you forward by providing actionable steps based on your current business and life goals.**

What do we mean by shifting your mindset?

I would dare say that you already have an empowering mindset in several areas of your life. If that weren't true, you wouldn't be reading this book. If asked, you could easily list areas where you've been consistently proactive, intentional, and thriving. This is not the mindset you need to shift.

I would also dare to say that you have at least one area of your life that is *less empowering* than you would like. On the contrary, you feel like you're losing in this area rather than winning. Honestly, it's difficult for you to accept.

You undoubtedly succeed in so many areas, but this one is the clear exception. When you look back at your mindset—in addition to your results—it troubles you. Your thoughts about this issue are often reactive, timid, and disempowering.

Why would this one area of your life be the anomaly for your life? What does it benefit you to succeed in so many areas but constantly fail at this one area?

And that, my friend, is why I became a professional coach. This is exactly where an experienced coach can make all the difference.

When you're fearful, passive, or neglectful in one area of your life, it affects *every* area of your life.

You might say, "Well, Marcel, that's not me. I'm not afraid of anything or anyone." I hear what you're saying, but fears are often dressed up as recurring problems and obstacles. Do you have any of those?

"One significant statistic as it relates to shifting your mindset is that individuals who have a growth mindset (the belief that abilities can be developed through effort) are more likely to achieve greater success in their personal and professional lives compared to those with a fixed mindset (the belief that abilities are fixed and cannot be changed). According to research by Carol Dweck, a Stanford University psychologist, **people with a growth mindset tend to be more open to challenges, more resilient in the face of setbacks, and more motivated to learn and improve.**"[5]

---

[5] Dweck, Carol S. Mindset: The New Psychology of Success. Random House, 2006, p.35

This is where a shift in mindset can make huge gains in your life. If your life has been running well on seven out of eight cylinders, how would it help you to find greater clarity and direction on the eighth cylinder?

The more you succeed, the easier it is to hide.

I have the privilege of coaching some of the most successful people in executive leadership. Here's an unfortunate reality. The higher you rise in executive leadership, the easier it becomes to *ignore* areas of your life that require more attention.

I'm not talking about some horrible crime or shameful sin. I'm referring to disempowering mindsets that continuously serve as barriers in your life. With both ease and precision, they regularly block any forward momentum you attempt to gain.

And since the rest of your life is an obvious success, you can choose *not* to address this issue and be just fine—at least, that's what you've been telling yourself.

Develop a growth mindset in EVERY area of your life.

It should get better over time, right? It really doesn't affect any other area of my life, right? It won't get better automatically. It never does. To make matters worse, it always affects other areas of your life in more ways than you can imagine.

After working with exceptional—and highly capable—executive leaders, I've found one recurring theme. They do a great job leading from their strengths, **but they seldom take the time to honestly evaluate what keeps blocking them** from reaching their next level of success in their personal performance, with their teams, or in their family life.

Honestly evaluate your path

How do you replace disempowering fears—the mindset that holds you back from thriving in key areas of your life—with empowering confidence? The answer: *Shift* your mindset. This is the path of wisdom.

If communication with your team repeatedly falls flat, shift your mindset. If maximizing your time is a constant source of frustration, shift your mindset.

If the stress of your upcoming presentation to your investors is causing you to lose sleep, shift your mindset.

If you're paralyzed with indecision due to unexpected cost increases, shift your mindset. If the impasse in your marriage is damaging your relationship, shift your mindset.

When your largest client threatens to leave in 30 days unless you slash your prices—don't panic—shift your mindset.

Which of these key areas would be at the top of your list? What else would be a key factor?

And what else?

Now that you got that out of the way, let's carve a path forward. Although there are several steps in the process of shifting your mindset—this is where coaching comes in—let me give you the one that launches all others in the right direction.

Clarify what is true right now

Clarity is the *gateway* to shifting your mindset. Ask yourself the following questions as you seek to replace disempowering fears—obstacles, difficulties, challenges, or recurring problems—with *empowering* confidence.

The questions may relate to one or more people or a specific situation.

What's true about this right now?

What else is true?

What's my end goal?

What's important about this now?

What keeps getting in the way?

What else keeps getting in the way?

What have I done about this issue in the past?

What can I do about it now?

What else can I do about it?

And what else can I do about it?

Each question provides you with greater clarity.

Gaining greater clarity on the source of your recurring challenges is foundational to their resolution.

Clarity and empowering confidence are directly proportional to one another. **The more you explore, clarify, and reflect on their source, the more confidence you develop to act decisively.**

This is how you begin to shift your mindset.

The Coaching Advantage

Advantage #2

"Schreiner, in his work on Coaching Executives to Success, provides a thorough review of executive coaching research, highlighting its potential benefits for leaders, such as improved self-awareness, communication skills, and job satisfaction."[6]

---

[6] Schreiner, W. (2021). Coaching Executives to Success: A Review of Executive Coaching Research. Journal of Business and Psychology, 36(2), 255-278.

Mark's Coaching Advantage

When I first met Mark, I was struck by his glowing smile and genuine care for others. Mark's presence could neutralize any situation and turn things in the right direction within a few minutes.

Mark was more talented than he or his leaders at the university realized. This was especially true with Mark's department leader. Mark was not a political person but worked in a political environment.

After fighting several battles—all of which he lost—to improve his team's performance, Mark resigned and looked for other opportunities.

When Mark and I met for coaching, he was discouraged and dejected. Mark wanted to move forward, but his previous experience left him feeling unworthy of greater positions.

Replace Disempowering Fears with Empowering Confidence

As we worked through what Mark wanted his future to look like, Mark's eyes lit up again with great enthusiasm. Mark was excited about what could be and should be. But Mark's disempowering thoughts *limited* his potential—and his decisions—in many frustrating ways.

As we worked through Mark's disempowering thoughts and reflections, Mark experienced a new infusion of hope for what was possible. Mark was not the one who lost. It was the university that lost an exceptional leader before their time.

Mark was not the incompetent factor in the equation. His boss was the one totally clueless about how to increase performance and realize greater employee engagement. Mark was a winner. His boss was the loser.

There was nothing Mark could do about his past, but there was a great deal available to do in the present. Was it painful? Without question. Was it unjust what Mark experienced? Absolutely. The fact remained; it was time to *move forward*.

> **There are crucial moments in your life when only one question must be asked, "Am I going to live stuck in my past—defeated, deflated, and disempowered—or empowered and action-focused to build my future?"**

When I asked, "Mark, what can you do about it now?" this was the moment everything changed. Mark reflected, "I can't do anything to change what they did to me, but I can start something new right now," and he did.

Questions like "What else can you do about it?" and "What's important to you about this right now?" narrowed down our focus. Each question provided Mark with greater clarity.

As we continued to meet and engage at deeper levels, Mark eventually applied for an executive position at another university. His confidence shifted upwards, and he followed through on a solid course of action. And guess what? Mark got the job!

Move Forward   Lead Confidently   Accelerate Performance

Questions for Reflection

1. How would you define the word mindset?

2. What empowering mindset exists today in a key area of your life?

3. What factors make them a permanent fixture in your mind?

4. What disempowering mindset exists today in a key area of your life?

5. What has contributed to maintaining this perspective in your life?

6. On a scale from 1-10, with 10 representing maximum clarity, how much clarity do you have regarding the source of your recurring challenges?

7. "The more you succeed, the easier it is to hide." What's true about this statement in your life right now?

Chapter 3

Get Yourself Out of the Way

Accelerate Your Performance From Good to Great

Move Forward   Lead Confidently   Accelerate Performance

Exposing Coaching Myths

Myth #3 – Coaching is only for people that have difficult problems.

The Real Story

Coaching does so much more. It focuses on helping successful people—just like you—**overcome** recurring obstacles and disempowering mindsets to **move from good to great** in your relationships, throughout your business, and with your most important goals.

You have areas in your life that are good, but not great. These areas may be acceptable, but they're far from exceptional.

Although you may point to many factors that influence this reality—one thing is crystal clear—*you* are the primary factor and influencer in your performance.

In the previous chapter, we highlighted the importance of exploring, clarifying, and reflecting on the source of your recurring challenges. In this chapter, we want to accentuate the importance of taking *ownership* and assuming *full* responsibility for your performance.

This isn't anything new, right? You make this a non-negotiable for your executive leaders and staff. You run weekly reports to make sure your clients are performing as agreed.

You preach responsibility and performance to your children often. And you challenge those in your community to take responsibility for their community.

But what about you?

Do you *consistently* practice what you preach?

Have you gotten so comfortable with measuring the performance of others that you've *neglected* to measure and improve your own performance?

As the leader—like it or not—you're an example for others to study and follow.

You're an example of integrity, justice, and diligence.

You're an example of a disciplined life.

You're an example of initiative and service.

You're an example of treating others with respect and kindness.

And among these character qualities and others, you're an example of personal sacrifice for the benefit of others.

I know. I know. You didn't sign up for all this. But, when you decided to lead others, you also signed up to model a higher standard.

And, like it or not, you're responsible for getting better in each of these areas. But wait, there's more.

On top of all these expectations—and without sacrificing your character in the process—you're *exclusively* responsible for improving your performance. But you won't get better unless you assume full ownership of your performance.

What exactly does that mean? Don't assign blame to your team for their performance. *Own* the shortfall yourself.

"Coaching clients are some of the happiest clients on the planet. Here's a wild discovery: 99% of individuals and companies who decide to hire a coach are "satisfied or very satisfied" and 96% say they would hire a coach again."[7]

---

[7] https://www.ipeccoaching.com/hubfs/What%20is%20Coaching%20-%20iPEC%20Coach%20Training.pdf

Don't blame your client for their abrupt decision to walk away. Start introspecting instead. And please, don't unleash your frustration on your spouse in a single conversation. They deserve better than that.

When you decided to lead others, you also signed up to model a higher standard.

By now, you've surely concluded one thing in life. You can't control what others think, speak, or act, but you can control what you do in each of these areas.

Let's review.

How do you get yourself out of the way?

You get yourself out of the way by taking complete ownership of your performance while assuming full responsibility for your results.

But wait… there's one more point to add.

You get yourself out of the way by presenting the *best* version of yourself as the way to increase your performance.

This is short for self-awareness. Through coaching, you gain greater clarity in key areas where you have settled for what's good without a plan to make it great.

The International Coaching Federation (ICF) provides us with the following statistics on the benefits of executive coaching:

70% Increase in Individual Performance

- Goal Attainment
- Clearer Communication
- Higher Satisfaction

50% Increase in Team Performance

- Better Conversations
- Improved Collaboration
- Enhanced Work Performance

48% Increase in Organizational Performance

- Increase in Revenue
- Increase in Employee Retention
- Customers as Advocates[8]

---

[8] https://www.american.edu/provost/ogps/executive-education/executive-coaching/roi-of-executive-coaching.cfm

If you need more experience, get more experience. Don't complain about your lack of experience. Stop whining about what you should've done in the past. It's too late. You can't get on a time machine and change the past.

Get yourself out of the way, by presenting the best version of yourself as the way to increase your performance.

Instead, honestly evaluate your current gaps and plan to get them filled in sooner rather than later. That, my friend, is productive thinking. And that kind of thinking will move your life *forward*.

If you need better tools, get better tools. There's so much available today to get you from where you are to where you want to be. There's simply no excuse to remain stuck in any area of life. You literally have a treasure of information right at your fingertips as you search for information online.

If you need advanced training, sign up for that next course, webinar, workshop, or intensive. Stop thinking about it and just do it.

And if you want to get better, faster—and accelerate those areas presently on hold in your life—hire a Certified Professional Coach.

What's the implication?

I'm so glad you asked!

You are the driver of your performance. You set the vision, and you establish the goals. You get the training, and you buy the tools. You take the initiative, and you set the pace. You leverage your resources, and you hire the coach.

And you commit all you've got—focus, energy, time, strength, resources, etc.—to get the extraordinary results you really want.

You are the one who must shift your mindset

You are the one that can work smarter and not harder. You are the one that must empower your executive team.

You are the one that can break the plateau in your marriage and be fully present with your spouse and with your children.

So, what exactly are you removing in the process? You're removing your pride and the limiting beliefs that you raise up to "protect" you from what most intimidates you. Stop trying to be "perfect" in what you're doing. It simply won't happen.

Do better than good at what you do. Be the best version of yourself. This is how you *accelerate* your performance from good to great. This is how you achieve *synergy* in your work life and your family life.

And when you—as the leader—accelerate your performance, it will raise the bar with your executive leaders, staff, and employees. It will infuse new life into your marriage and family life. It will expand your vision of what should and could be. All of this is possible because the *good* has now become *great*.

And this is one of the key reasons I became a Certified Professional Coach. It's because so many high-capacity leaders have *parked* their performance in the good parking lot rather than where they can experience true greatness. Is that you?

"Today, driven entrepreneurs possess more potential to excel. Meanwhile, many of them are not coming close to realizing their full potential. **Business coaching can help entrepreneurs break through barriers that are holding them back and focus on the actions necessary to achieve their goals.** In addition, many business owners now have tremendous interest in investing in coaching for their leadership teams to improve the performance of everyone at their companies resulting in greater synergistic success."[9]

---

[9] https://www.forbes.com/sites/russalanprince/2018/10/08/why-business-coaching-is-booming/?sh=337b5df720ff

Exposing Coaching Myths

Myth #4 – Coaching only works if the coach and the client have similar experiences.

The Real Story

Effective coaching just works. Your coach doesn't have to have similar experiences in relationships, health, business, goals, education, or other areas to walk with you from where you are to where you want to be.

The Coaching Advantage

Advantage #3

"Executive coaching can help leaders foster innovation in high-tech firms. Coaching can help leaders develop their creativity, strategic thinking, and risk-taking abilities, which are critical for driving innovation and staying competitive in fast-paced industries."[10]

---

[10] Anderson, M., & Day, D. (2020). Coaching executives for innovation: Insights from high-tech firms. Journal of Business Research, 113, 348-357.

Esther's Coaching Advantage

Esther's character could be marked by one word—service. She was always willing and available to serve others. After working through an extremely painful divorce, Esther was in a serious slump. Her co-workers knew it, her friends knew it, I knew it, and Esther knew it as well.

Although Esther had always performed at her very best at work, with friends, and at her church responsibilities, every area of her life had started a downward spiral.

Esther wanted to change, but she didn't know where to begin. This is not an uncommon reality in today's world.

Esther wanted to shift her perspective and change her performance. She had grown too comfortable with only doing things "good enough" to get by as she worked through her losses.

To realize change, Esther needed to get herself out of the way and change her performance expectations. She needed accountability, and she needed clear goals. Esther had neither, at least not until we started our sessions.

Accelerate Your Performance From Good to Great

So, what do you do when your world—and your future—have been derailed by relational loss?

What happens when everything you've hoped for is no longer on the horizon?

You get yourself out of the way by taking complete ownership of your performance while assuming full responsibility for your results.

This is how you increase your performance. This is how you start to get better faster. And as Esther came to discover—through our coaching process—you gain greater clarity in the things that matter most in your life when you *don't* settle for what's good enough but on what's best.

Esther was the one that needed to change her mindset.

Esther was the one that needed to get unstuck from what was "good" to get to what was "great."

Esther was the one that needed to assume full ownership—extreme ownership—for her *effort* and for her *results*.

Esther had the capacity to move things forward.

Esther had the skills to get her from where she was to where she wanted to be.

Esther alone could accelerate her performance, not because she had to, but because now, she *wanted* to change and was *ready* to make changes.

And all of this was possible because Esther partnered with an experienced coach. She did not always like what was said, where it was said, or how it was said.

But deep down inside, Esther was clear on one thing. If she wanted to get from where she was to where she wanted to be, *intentional action* would need to become the new norm in her life.

Questions for Reflection

1. What key area of your life needs to move from good to great?

2. What do you believe is the root cause for not moving forward sooner? What got in the way?

3. What's the primary concern behind your answer?

4. What training or experience do you need to get you there?

5. What's the main thing that keeps getting in the way of your success?

6. What else keeps getting in the way?

7. We mentioned three essential requirements to get yourself out of the way—ownership, responsibility, and self-awareness. What changes in these three areas are needed right now?

Chapter 4

Don't Sabotage Your Marriage

Intentionally Direct, Protect, and Grow your Marriage

Exposing Coaching Myths

Myth #5 – Coaching only helps business leaders to reach their professional development goals.

The Real Story

Coaching will help you move forward in other key areas, such as health, community, personal vision and mission, planning, education, career, family, church, and marriage.

I must confess something here. Marriage and family are two of my favorite topics. Why? Because only second to my faith, my relationship with Yami, Luke, and Savanah is a top priority for me.

Your marriage *matters*, and so do your children. Let's start first with your marriage. By the way, if you're a single business professional, I hope this chapter will encourage you to remain steadfast as you wait for God to provide you with a godly spouse.

Now, back to the marriage matters part. I've spent more than half of my adult life coaching married business professionals. I must admit, you can really make a mess of your marriage relationship.

What's worse, you can devastate your spouse, crush their spirit, and wreck your home, all in less than 60 minutes.

It can happen, and it does happen. Highly driven and future-thinking people just like you wreck their marriages all the time.

It's painful to watch others experience this in their marriage. It's even worse when your marriage implodes and falls apart.

But can you really thrive in business *and* your marriage? Can you discover new and effective ways to prioritize your marriage? Yes! These are possible but never easy. And one more thing. Seldom do you figure out how all on your own.

Imagine you're at the office for a moment. You've wrestled with a decision that will positively affect one manager and devastate another manager. Regardless of what you choose, it will affect one manager or the other.

You decide on a course of action. The decision is now final. Prior to implementing this decision, you contact both managers involved. You advise them of your decision and begin to explore new methods.

They both agree that problems will evolve from this decision. Still, they're *committed* to building a culture of respect, trust, and communication to defend against these inevitable issues once they surface.

The same is true in your marriage.

The decisions you make today in your marriage will always create relational ripples—or challenges—in your marriage. Even good decisions can create difficulties for you and your spouse to work through.

"There are so many benefits to coaching. Would these benefits not transfer to busy business professionals that want to grow their marriage? Of course, they would. Coaching brings out the best in individuals. It can do the same for couples in their marriage too. Ken Blanchard reminds us of the powerful impact of coaching on the lives of busy professionals. Coaching evokes new skills, increased behavioral knowledge, valuable experiences, goal-orientation, self-reliance, increased responsibility, more productivity, better commitments, and higher levels of satisfaction."[11]

---

[11] Ken Blanchard, "Managing Coaching for Results and ROI," (Escondido: The Ken Blanchard Companies, 2021), page 4. Ken Blanchard, "Managing Coaching for Results and ROI," (Escondido: The Ken Blanchard Companies,

Knowing how to address these ripples in your relationship *early*—before they evolve into larger waves of problems—can serve as an ever-increasing line of defense for your marriage.

Your marriage is worth the investment of all that you've got.

Is your marriage built to last? Do you invest *more* money in your professional development than your marriage development?

You develop your soft skills, so why not develop your marriage skills?

You arrive early and work late to make sure everything is running smoothly at the office, so why not readjust your schedule to make sure that your marriage is getting the time it needs to flourish?

You plan annual executive retreats with your team, so why not plan a marriage retreat with your spouse?

Casting vision, formulating strategies, and effective planning are essential to the long-term health of your business. Could your marriage benefit from this intentional three-fold focus?

You must invest generously in your marriage to strengthen and grow your relationship.

2021), 4, https://resources.kenblanchard.com/whitepapers/managing-coaching-for-results-and-roi.

You constantly watch online webinars and training courses, so why not consider an online marriage course? If it's important to develop your business skills to succeed in your professional life, how much more important is it to develop your relational skills to grow in your marriage life?

You might've considered coaching to accelerate your business performance. Why not consider a marriage coach to accelerate your marriage relationship?

What does it help your business to remain in a passive posture while watching your competition gain market share?

It doesn't help you at all.

What does it help your marriage to remain in a passive posture while doing nothing proactive to direct, protect, or grow your marriage skills?

You guessed it!

It doesn't help your marriage at all.

I'm sure you see where I'm going here.

If you're not generously investing time, money, energy, planning, and other resources to develop your marriage—as you instinctively do to build your business—**the evidence is indisputable and clear: you love your business more than you love your spouse. And when you arrive at this point in your life, there's a high probability that you will do something stupid and sabotage your marriage.**

Catch stupid early! Stop it from wrecking your life and your marriage!

Sin makes you stupid!

Stupid does not discriminate. Young and old, educated and non-educated, rich and poor, brown and tan, black and white, short and tall, single and married, religious and irreligious, all have the same capacity to be stupid.

In church circles, a popular phrase reads, "Sin makes you stupid." I must confess something here. I really hate the word stupid, but I absolutely love this phrase! I've seen the pattern reveal itself consistently in the lives of people.

In this context, sin is anything you do that *contradicts* God's Word—the Bible. For example, if you lie, whether the color of that lie is white, yellow, green, or some other color—as if lies had any color at all—it is considered a sin and must be confessed.

All of us are guilty of breaking one of God's holy commandments in thought, word, or deed. I'm certainly at the front of the sin line. And I believe you might be standing next to me. Smile.

Since I also serve as an Executive Pastor, my theological hat is always close by. More on that later. Now, let's get back to stupid.

Is it really an innocent mistake?

Pay close attention here. Getting off on the wrong exit, not reviewing your presentation before meeting with your client, or ordering something you're allergic to because you neglected to read the explanation on the menu is an innocent oversight.

You may call it an error or a mistake, but it's certainly not in the *sin* category. Lying to your spouse about the request made by the person that sat with you over lunch—enticing you to "quietly adjust the numbers" for the sake of the investors—is not an innocent oversight or the result of a new clever malware-creating computer problem.

It's a clear invitation to sin and add more makeup to an ugly frog.

Is it an accident?

Nope.

Is the problem so complicated that no one can get to the root cause of the poor quarterly performance report?

I seriously doubt it.

Be honest with your spouse in all things, in every inquiry, and always. Your spouse is the primary person in your life to help you *identify* stupid early and *stop* it. Don't shut them down. *Listen* to their perspective on the matter. Don't be stupid in your marriage.

You can't consistently lie to your spouse and simultaneously build your marriage.

"When both husband and wife fully commit to marriage coaching to grow their relationship, both will benefit, and both will be positively influenced by this commitment. According to Relational-Cultural Theory, in a growth-fostering relationship, both people are open to being influenced and changed by the other."[12]

This is the power behind marriage coaching. Not only can it bring couples together to focus on their relationship, but it can also evoke the required energy and personal will to implement new and collaborative approaches to relational transformation.

---

[12] Judith Jordan, Relational–cultural theory: The power of connection to transform our lives. The Journal of Humanistic Counseling, 56(3), (2017) 228-243. https://onlinelibrary.wiley.com/doi/abs/10.1002/johc.12055. (Accessed December 21, 2021).

Entering the hotel room of a colleague—that, by the way, has told you repeatedly how very attractive you look during the conference—to have a few drinks and "talk business" is not an error, and it's certainly not a careless oversight; it's totally stupid, and it will lead you to sin.

Notice the downward progression. You believe that you're *that* attractive. You swallow the hook, the line, the sinker, the shiny lure, and the fishing rod too. You don't see this as a threat to your marriage but as a boost to your already hyper-inflated ego.

After all, it's about time someone noticed—since you think your wife doesn't notice—how well you take care of your body, what great hair you have, and how unusually well you dress for your age—whatever that means.

Can you see how sin would make you move way beyond stupid in this scenario?

Stupid #1 - You believe the lie.

Stupid #2 - You agree to meet alone.

Stupid #3 - You dress provocatively to meet with this person that finds you very attractive.

Stupid #4 - You deceive yourself into believing that work matters will be the agenda for the evening.

Stupid #5 - You deliberately visit their room, close the door, and start flirting like a passionate dancer.

"What married couple would not benefit from increased passion, clarity, and action? What relationship would find fault in having more accurate self-awareness or greater self-worth?

As married couples begin marriage coaching, studies reveal that they can expect to gain greater inner awareness and new approaches to what's not working in their lives.

What does this do long-term? Married couples improve their communication skills, manage day-to-day life better, increase relational and personal confidence, and build new soft skills."[13]

---

[13] What is Coaching? Everything You've Wanted to Know, (iPec Coaching) December 21, 2021, https://www.ipeccoaching.com/hubfs/What%20is%20Coaching%20-%20iPEC%20Coach%20Training.pdf

Stupid #6 - You intentionally plan to get very comfortable with alcohol.

Stupid #7 - Talking turns to drinking, drinking turns to dancing, dancing turns to kissing, kissing turns to touching, and the rest is history.

None of this is innocent anything. Telling your spouse that this was only a one-time mistake would grossly insult their intelligence.

Don't insult them.

Call it what it is—*sin*.

And each sin you practice makes you more stupid than the prior sin.

It's like getting a stupid badge, except there's no celebration, banquet, or awards assembly. There's only relational destruction, broken promises, and an overwhelming amount of pain and suffering.

Please, don't sabotage your marriage.

Please, don't be stupid in your marriage.

**Sin makes you stupid.
It always has, and it always will.
When you get comfortable
with stupid, you sin more.**

Marriage coaches can help busy and aspiring business professionals by serving as "skilled coaches" in their relational development and personal growth.

These coaches stir what's uncomfortable to evoke what's possible.

As relational surgeons, marriage coaches carefully collaborate with their clients to remove annoying obstacles, such as limiting beliefs, while introducing new possibilities and sustainable hope for the future of their relationship.

Making sin-centered decisions

What's stupid in our context? Stupid is when you make *self*-centered decisions—which I call *sin*-centered decisions—to satisfy three key desires.

1. **The desires of your flesh** - A self-gratifying desire to please your body sexually outside of God's plan for marriage. It includes getting drunk, pornography, drug abuse, and others.

2. **The lust of your eyes** - A visually satisfying desire that leads you to obsess about having something that doesn't belong to you. Increasing jealousy, envy, and greed consume your thinking.

3. **The pride of your life** - An obsession with obtaining more power, authority, control, and attention to self. Here you're blinded by your own destructive ambitions and pursuits. In this third category, you do whatever it takes to reach the top.

Why is stupid so dangerous?

The more you sin, the more stupid you become. It's just that simple. As stupid increases so does the size of the wrecking ball that crashes against your spouse and others that you love.

Stupid—sin-centered—motives lead you to dwell on *unwise* thoughts. Unwise thoughts lead you to develop short-term thinking, which ultimately seeks to satisfy what you want right now, irrespective of the cost to your spouse and children.

Short-term thinking and living for the satisfaction of the here and now leads you to speak foolishly. At this point, wisdom is clearly lacking. People are shocked by the words that are coming out of your mouth, and it's not a good shock to their system.

Remember the timeless principle taught by Jesus: "For out of the abundance of the heart the mouth speaks." (Matthew 12:34)

To reiterate, your words most certainly spring forth from the generous content overflow of your heart.

Lastly, once your foolish speaking becomes the new pattern of your life, action follows close behind. Ultimately, sin's desire is for you to act on the stupidity of your motives.

Sin leads you slowly, methodically, and masterfully down a path of personal and relational destruction.

Don't be stupid in your marriage. Catch stupid *early* and stop it before it wrecks your life.

Are you ready for some good news? Here it goes…

Your marriage doesn't have to be bad to get better.

You *don't* have to be stupid in your marriage.

Do you believe this?

If you do, there's more good news.

You're 100% right. It doesn't.

You want your business to shift from good to great. You want this for every team, solution, and product. You don't want to limit what your business can do; you want to continue expanding and developing new ways to serve your clients.

You're not simply building a business—it's so much more than that—you want to build a legacy that makes an impact beyond your lifetime.

And if you work so hard to achieve this in your business, how much more *work* should you put into your marriage to leave a legacy with your spouse, children, extended family, and community?

And here's the good news.

You don't have to do this alone.

Your marriage doesn't have to be bad to get better, and your relationship doesn't have to crash and burn before you start *growing* your marriage skills.

Like most top-performing athletes, musicians, doctors, vocalists, public speakers, consultants, educators, and business leaders, you can lean on an experienced coach to walk with you through the intentional process of directing, protecting, and growing your marriage.

Remember, you don't have to do this alone.

Permission to walk together

On a practical level, marriage coaching is where you give me permission to walk together—with you and your spouse—to assess three key questions:

1. Where is your marriage *today*?

2. Where do you want your marriage relationship to be in the *future*?

3. What keeps getting in the *way* of your marriage goals, the future you both desire?

It's that simple.

And yet, every year, countless married business professionals invest thousands of dollars on amazing vacations while spending zero on developing relational skills to make their marriage thrive.

Does that resonate with your marriage relationship?

Think about it another way.

What is the maximum daily dollar amount you would be willing to set aside daily to take the most amazing two-week vacation with your spouse?

Would it be $500.00, $1,000.00, or $5,000.00 or more?

What is the maximum daily dollar amount that you would be willing to set aside every day to make sure that you remain in good health?

What's your daily number?

Would it be $500.00, $1,000.00, or $5,000.00 or more?

Lastly, what is the maximum daily dollar amount that you would be willing to set aside every day to make sure that your marriage thrives?

What's your daily number? Would it be $500.00, $1,000.00, or $5,000.00 or more?

Except for the best two-week vacation ever, your health and marriage don't have a maximum daily dollar amount.

Why not?

Because your health and your marriage are *priceless*. Assuming that your healthcare is covered, start investing in the relational *vitality* of your marriage.

There's no measure of energy too great. There's no stopwatch to race against. There's no such thing as *too much time*—neither quantity nor quality of time. And there will be no limit to your *commitment* nor to your investment of money. Why not?

You already know the answer.

Move Forward   Lead Confidently   Accelerate Performance

Your spouse is immeasurable, invaluable, priceless, and irreplaceable; they're worth every investment of time, energy, planning, focus, and all other resources that you have available to direct, protect, and grow your marriage.

Does online marriage coaching work as an effective modality?

Distanced-based coaching—although perceived as negative for some regarding personalization and engagement—is a more *favorable* factor in the coaching process than a less favorable factor. The benefits of in-person coaching are numerous indeed, but let's not discount the online benefits too quickly. There is no "one-size-fits-all" to coaching.

The effectiveness of marriage coaching is not measured by the modality of coaching but rather by the effectiveness in helping you and your spouse move forward along your relational journey.

Can you find compassion, empathy, acknowledgment, and coaching presence through video-based platforms? Yes, absolutely. Can online marriage coaching combined with online training help you and your spouse explore deeper levels of self-awareness and evoke new possibilities for your relationship? Yes, absolutely.

These experiences have been documented regularly in marriage therapy sessions *and* marriage coaching sessions as well. Sometimes for coaches and their clients, "distance" can be a good partner.

Online marriage coaching can facilitate deeper levels of self-awareness through the sheer distance and safety of the coaching engagement and process. Clients have reported feeling an *increased* sense of comfort and control—which has led to many positive outcomes—with the entire process of online coaching.[14] The benefits for married couples are indeed many.

And that's why I decided to serve as a marriage coach and create several online marriage courses—in English and in Spanish—to serve busy, faith-based business professionals who are *ready* to build their marriage and realize the life of their dreams.

Can online marriage coaching serve as an effective alternative to in-person marriage coaching?

The answer is a definitive "Yes!" As we conclude, let's summarize several key benefits as they relate to online marriage coaching and self-paced online learning for married couples.

- Increased space to carefully process marriage training videos in private before engaging with a marriage coach.

---

[14] Andrea Kysely et al., "Expectations and Experiences of Couples Receiving Therapy Through Videoconferencing: A Qualitative Study.," Frontiers in Psychology 10 (2019): 2992, https://doi.org/10.3389/fpsyg.2019.02992. (Accessed December 21, 2021).

- Elevated levels of self-awareness and personal reflection is evoked.

- Greater levels of coach and coachee accountability is realized.

- Relational satisfaction levels increased.

- Resistant spouses have obstacles to marriage coaching removed.

- Self-paced learning is taken seriously.

- Married couples can be coached from anywhere in the world.

- An environment of trust and safety is quickly realized.

- Sessions are profound and emotionally impactful.

- Session outcomes are obtained.

- Relational passion, self-confidence, and communication skills thrive.

- Work/life balance, work performance, and time management flourish.

- New patterns of thinking emerge.

Experience the life of your dreams

Can marriage coaching serve to *grow* your marriage and help you and your spouse experience the life of your dreams?

You bet it can?

As I always say, you need three things to grow your marriage.

1. You need a **Commitment**

2. You need a **Coach**, and

3. You need a **Course of Action.**

If you and your spouse are committed to investing time, energy, focus, and resources to make your marriage thrive, marriage coaching may be just what you need to lead your marriage from a good marriage to a great marriage.

The Coaching Advantage

Advantage #4

"The benefits of marriage coaching for business leaders include improved communication, increased emotional intelligence, and better conflict resolution skills.

Investing in one's marriage can have a positive impact on one's business, as a healthy and supportive home life can help leaders be more focused and productive at work."[15]

---

[15] Geiger, J. (2021, January 27). The Benefits of Marriage Coaching for Business Leaders. Entrepreneur. Retrieved from https://www.entrepreneur.com/article/363078.

Robert and Maria's Coaching Advantage

What happens when you combine a driven business professional with a spouse that's also highly driven in their work? Both are ambitious, both are talented, and both excel in amazing ways. Although you get maximum productivity at work, you most certainly get a good measure of *conflict* at home.

That was Robert and Maria's story. At work, both were unstoppable. They were respected and admired by their peers. They made extraordinary contributions at the office, but their home life was totally different.

Don't Sabotage Your Marriage

At home, both were deeply frustrated, discouraged, and indifferent about their marriage. They had plenty of energy and drive for their business relationships, but their marriage relationship was in shambles.

Both Robert and Maria were sabotaging their marriage. They were building communication walls, hurting one another emotionally, neglecting each other sexually, and increasing their stress levels beyond what they had ever imagined.

Thankfully, they each had a generous measure of humility to reach out to me to begin our marriage coaching sessions. Humility is *key* to moving your marriage in the right direction.

I'm so glad that Robert and Maria took the first step. It was the perfect time to refresh, refocus, and reprioritize their relationship.

Intentionally direct, protect, and grow your marriage.

Robert and Maria committed to watching my online marriage course. They took the time to reflect and talk about what they learned in each session. This by itself remarkably improved their communication.

Once we connected on Zoom, Robert and Maria watched the videos, completed the activities, spent time reflecting and talking through what they'd learned, and had at least one week to process their progress.

At this point, my job consisted of helping them connect the dots, clarify what was learned, and draw out positive action steps to lead them from where they were to where they wanted to be.

Every marriage needs a commitment, a coach, and a course of action to grow, and to get better faster.

Today, Robert and Maria continue to perform at their peak performance at work *and* home. Once they started marriage coaching, they also welcomed their second child. They now serve one another in their relationship and continue to *thrive* at home.

Questions for Reflection

1. What are you communicating to your spouse from the level of *sacrifice* you make each day to serve them and meet their needs?

2. What one action step could you start today that would demonstrate a greater measure of love and respect for your spouse?

3. What do you need to adjust in your daily schedule to be more present with your spouse?

4. Where are you being stupid in your marriage?

5. What do you need to stop doing right now to avoid the slippery slope of stupidity and sin?

6. If your marriage is bad, what are you willing to do to make it better?

7. If your marriage is good, what are you willing to do to make it great?

Chapter 5

Be Present and Engaged With Your Children

Personally Love, Encourage, and Train Your Children

Exposing Coaching Myths

Myth #6 – Coaching is a collection of basic knowledge and opinions about human motivation mixed with modern approaches to mentoring and training.

The Real Story

Coaching is first client specific. The client and their specific goals and challenges are the agenda. Each coaching session is unique. There is no step-by-step formula to follow. Obviously, there are opinions, knowledge, and extensive research, but they are reserved by the coach. **You as the client are the only focus in the coaching session.**

Children are God's gifts to us and to the world. You will never be the "perfect parent," and neither will you be the "worst parent" on planet Earth.

Give yourself some slack, but not too much slack.

You can easily outsource specific talent to fill in the gaps in your business when the required skills don't exist in your business.

Need a programmer? No problem.

Need a new logo? No problem.

Need someone to translate your corporate policy into two additional languages? No problem.

Parenting is very different.

Your children need sacrificial love.

That's *your* job.

Love your children!

Love is foundational to effective parenting. When love is present, hope fills the environment; almost anything is possible. When love is absent, despair sets in; possibilities are significantly limited.

Consider the characteristics of love found within one of the most cherished scripture passages in all the Bible.

1 Corinthians 13:1-8

1 If I speak in the tongues of men and of angels, but have not love, I am a noisy gong or a clanging cymbal. **2** And if I have prophetic powers, and understand all mysteries and all knowledge, and if I have all faith, so as to remove mountains, but have not love, I am nothing. **3** If I give away all I have, and if I deliver up my body to be burned, but have not love, I gain nothing. **4** Love is patient and kind; love does not envy or boast; it is not arrogant **5** or rude. It does not insist on its own way; it is not irritable or resentful; **6** it does not rejoice at wrongdoing, but rejoices with the truth. **7** Love bears all things, believes all things, hopes all things, endures all things. **8** Love never ends.

Underline the characteristics of genuine love found in this remarkable passage. Take a minute to think deeply about these amazing qualities.

Are these qualities of love *consistently* practiced in your life?

Research has shown that parental involvement in children's lives can have positive effects on their social, emotional, and academic development, including:

- Improved academic performance and behavior in school
- Increased self-esteem and self-confidence
- Better mental health and reduced risk of substance abuse
- Stronger relationships with peers and adults
- Higher levels of empathy and compassion

It is important to note that while the benefits of parental involvement are clear, the specific ways parents can be involved can vary greatly depending on the child's age, interests, and needs.

Which characteristics of genuine love do you need to work on most regarding loving your spouse and children?

Which characteristic is most consistent in your life today?

Which one is your least consistent?

Which characteristic of love would you be able to do something about this week?

What will you do differently?

There's an important principle for you to consider seriously. The electrical connection between the two is nothing short of powerful.

Love and sacrifice are intimately connected.

The more you love your spouse and children, the more you will place their needs *ahead* of your own. Loving your children, although multidimensional, has sacrificial service at its core.

When love is present, sacrifice is deliberate. When love is absent, sacrifice is nowhere to be found.

Your children need to see you make regular sacrifices in your busy schedule for their benefit alone. As they get older, your children will quickly pick up when you're multitasking and not really present, though your body is close by.

Love your children unconditionally.

How do you do that?

First, love them because they're your children.

Tell them repeatedly about your great love for them. Remove every unrealistic expectation you've placed on them.

They will never be just like you. Do you really want another you in this world?

Second, love them *with* your words, emotions, and physical touch. Your words have a lifetime impact on your children. They will remember what you said and how you said it to them. They will remember your hugs and kisses and celebrations together.

Your children greatly need to hear how much you love them.
But also, they must feel your love emotionally and physically.

Tell your children just how much they mean to you with every opportunity.

Tell them how proud you are to be called their parent.

Tell them how much they delight your soul and bring joy to your heart.

Tell them how special they are to your family and the unique contribution they make to enrich others with their presence.

Tell them how confident you are about their future.

Tell them how much you love them and how you feel every time you think about them.

Tell them once, twice, 10,000 times per day if you have enough time and opportunity to do so.

Tell them that you love them when you wake up.

Tell them that you love them over breakfast.

Call them by phone and tell them you love them when you're on the road.

Send them a text and write, "I was just thinking about you. I love you!" Write them a note on a card as you express your love in creative ways. Tell them you love them over dinner and before they go to bed in the evening.

You get the point.

When you genuinely love your children—and they can *see* and *feel* your love—it's a *powerful moment*.

Third, your children need you to love them with your *presence*. Being present with your children communicates love in powerful ways.

You don't always have to solve every problem and deliver innovative solutions. Being present and listening well is often all that's needed.

There's nothing that encourages your children more than being fully present and engaged in what they love to do.

Move Forward   Lead Confidently   Accelerate Performance

Practical ways to be more present and engaged with your children

1. Plan long walks together
2. Plan activities together that they enjoy
3. Ask them regularly about their dreams and challenges
4. Go to their special events
5. Take trips together
6. Speak with them regularly
7. Model good behavior
8. Coach them to resolve conflicts and solve problems
9. Be available when they face difficult challenges
10. Show them how to serve
11. Teach them how to manage their finances
12. Teach them how to practice time maximization skills
13. Give them a measure of authority and responsibility
14. Teach them how to be kind, generous, and forgiving
15. Plan fun recreational activities together

Your children are yours to love, encourage, and train.

Your children need *authentic* encouragement, affirmation, and discipline. They really need you to cheer them on to do what is right. They can't see how talented they are, but you can. They don't always believe in their capacity to overcome the hurdles they face, but you can show them how to win in life and build greater confidence.

Encourage your children

Your children need *consistent* discipline to help them thrive as young people and as adults. Loving discipline is an *overflow* of your love for your children. Not disciplining your children is irresponsible. The opposite extreme is also irresponsible. Avoid both by always disciplining your children with a balance of truth and love.

Your children don't want a disengaged parent. No one benefits from that mindset. They need you to be *fully* present. They don't need a parent that is missing in action or unaware of important details that impact them daily.

Imagine if your top client wanted to meet with you in person for three hours without much notice. You would likely rearrange your schedule, prepare as much as possible, and take notes during your meeting. There would be no question at all pertaining to your level of engagement.

It would be at an all-time high. *Nothing* would distract you or pull you out of that meeting.

That's the type of commitment your spouse and children are looking for. They deserve nothing less.

And by the way, that's *your* job.

Train your children

Training is important for raising healthy and responsible children. What's required? Your children need a parent that is spiritually, physically, mentally, and emotionally present. There are no conference calls, no video meetings, no virtual reality, and no formal letters.

Parental training is hands-on training

Here's a simple model to help you encourage your children in the training process.

Explain, Model, Invite, and Coach

Tell them what work needs to be completed.

Tell them why the work needs to be completed.

Tell them how the work needs to be completed.

Show them how the work should be completed.

Ask if they have any questions about what they saw.

Invite them to join you in doing the work together.

Encourage them to work hard and with excellence.

Coach them on ways to improve their skills.

Point out areas done well and areas for improvement.

Model the methodology and skills once more.

Ask if they have any additional questions.

Invite them to do the work again by themselves.

Watch them work and continue to coach them to *perfect* their methodology and skills once completed.

As a relentlessly committed, fully present, and totally engaged parent, that's your job. You can't outsource what you're directly responsible for to others. It's your job to own and assume responsibility for.

And here is where coaching can serve you well. Among other benefits, coaching holds you accountable to *fulfill* the commitments you make to the people that matter most in your life.

And yes, your children, and the commitments you make to each one, are included to keep you focused on the right priorities for your life and family.

Your children need to learn how to honor God and love people. They need to see a good example of what it means to practice self-control, say no when necessary, manage money, schedule appointments, find directions, complete job applications, treat others respectfully, grow into responsible adults, and be aware of their surroundings.

As a parent, that's your job.

The Coaching Advantage

Advantage #5

"Executive coaching can help business leaders improve their work-life balance and reduce stress, which can, in turn, benefit their families and children. The study found that executive coaching helped leaders set boundaries between work and home life, prioritize family time, and manage their stress levels, which led to better physical and emotional health outcomes for themselves and their families."[16]

---

[16] O'Shea, D. (2021). The Impact of Executive Coaching on the Work-Life Balance of Business Leaders. Journal of Applied Psychology, 105(3), 245-257.

Steve's Coaching Advantage

There was not a single minute of wasted time on Steve's daily calendar. He managed to fill his calendar every day of the week. I must admit, after hearing about his schedule, I wondered when he had any time left for his wife and children.

And that's exactly what Steve wanted to talk about over a good cup of coffee. Steve came to the realization that he was *not* all-knowing. He knew that—although I wasn't the perfect father—I had extensive experience in this area of life.

You only have a window of time to invest in your children's lives. Refuse to build a collection of regrets. Invest generous amounts of time with your children—today.

As we engaged in our coaching session, Steve came to the realization that his presence was everywhere, but not with his children. He realized that his pace of work and life was *neither* sustainable nor healthy for his family.

Be Present and Engaged With Your Children

Steve deeply loved his wife and loved his children. He spoke highly of them in our session. His electric enthusiasm was noticeable.

He shared a few stories about his wife and how she gave up her career to focus on raising their kids. Steve talked about how much he loved to be around his kids. There was just one problem. Steve's presence at home more reflected a *traveler* on the go than it did a committed husband and father.

Personally Love, Encourage, and Train Your Children

Steve arrived at a point in our conversation that changed everything. Through a series of open-ended questions, Steve came to the realization that it was *possible* to change his schedule and maximize the time he spent investing in his wife and children.

What Steve had neglected to fully grasp prior to our coaching session was that he was the one *responsible* for his schedule. Steve was the one who overbooked his calendar. He was the one that was not present. And Steve was the only one who could change what happened after our session.

So many times during my coaching sessions, I see people believe the lie that they have no control over their present situation. They say, "That's the way it is, and I have to accept it," which is not reality at all. It's a lie, and we buy into this lie every day when we refuse to consider another perspective.

And once again, here's where coaching makes the difference. Coaching gets in your business and challenges your thinking. Coaching focuses on your goals and dreams. It helps you to clearly see what's really getting in the way. And if coaching helped Steve, it can serve you in the same way.

Move Forward   Lead Confidently   Accelerate Performance

Questions for Reflection

1. What are you communicating to your children from the level of sacrifice you make each day to serve them and meet their needs?

2. What insecurities do your children have? How can you infuse greater confidence in these areas?

3. What one action step could you start today that would demonstrate a greater measure of love and respect for your children?

4. What do you need to adjust in your daily schedule to be more present with your children?

5. What can you do today to love your children more meaningfully?

6. What can you do—practically speaking—to encourage and train your children this week?

7. What can you do with your children today to increase laughter and fun in the relationship?

Chapter 6

Stop Being Lazy and Start Moving Forward

*Leverage Discipline
to Advance Through
Your Obstacles*

Exposing Coaching Myths

Myth #7 – Coaching requires at least 12-18 months of intense weekly coaching sessions prior to seeing any visible results.

The Real Story

That is certainly an exaggeration if applied to every coaching client. I've seen clients gain powerful awareness about a challenge they wanted to explore, shift their mindset after deep reflection, and start experiencing visible results in less than three sessions. And if others experienced this change, so can you.

Obstacles in your life serve as a constant reminder of the imperfect world you enthusiastically call your home.

Some obstacles arrive with a warning sign—you can plan for their arrival—while others come as a complete surprise. Some obstacles are predictable, while others are not very predictable at all.

What relationship exists between the obstacles you face every day and the subject of personal discipline? Does living a disciplined life really matter?

Yes, it does.

Can being disciplined help you overcome predictable and unpredictable obstacles?

Yes, it can.

My hope is that you would discover and practice the surprising advantage of starting *small*—making small, measurable, and attainable commitments— and find increasingly fulfilling benefits as you commit to small improvements to overcome obstacles and move your life forward.

"Coaching is unlocking a person's potential to maximize their own performance. It is helping them to learn rather than teaching them."
– John Whitmore[17]

"Discipline is just choosing between what you want now and what you want most." – Unknown

---

[17] Whitmore, John. Coaching for Performance: Growing People, Performance, and Purpose. Nicholas Brealey Publishing, 2005.

Plan, start, and execute better

Maybe I offended you when you read "Stop Being Lazy" in this chapter title. My intent is not to offend but to *evoke* something within you.

Instinctively—like most people reading this book—the thought, "I'm definitely *not* a lazy person," flashed in your mind.

Let me clarify what I mean in this context. You have goals and dreams that you want to reach. This is the desired destination. For now, you find yourself somewhere short of this destination. This point of reference is the starting point of your gap.

The gap is what prevents you from getting from where you are to where you want to be in life.

The gap is very real, but it is *not* reduced automatically. The implication is that you first must identify where you stand—the point of departure—before you can make any concrete plans to measure and advance.

When I visited the London Underground, my good friend Ryan explained a simple phrase, "Mind the gap," that is announced when you're about to board a train.

The phrase serves as a warning and as a reminder. It reminds you to pay attention to where you're standing, see the gap that exists before boarding the train, and be careful as you board or disembark from the train.

When I coach and train others on how to develop the habit of extraordinary discipline in areas such as their spiritual life, relationships, health, education, goals, and others, I help them to identify three critical points of reference:

1. **Where are they right now? This is the starting point. It clearly defines today's reality.**

2. **Where do they want to be? This represents the client's big dream or destination.**

3. **What separates the two? This is the distance or gap that exists between the two.**

What surprises most of my clients is when I add the word "lazy" in relation to their gap. When compared to other high-performing areas of their lives—which, by the way, have a highly disciplined practice—there's often a *sharp* contrast with these not-so-great areas.

So often, the questions I ask serve to uncover the root cause of this dilemma. Because it is so inconsistent with other areas of their lives, we must explore what's getting in the way of their performance.

The same would apply to you.

"Discipline is the bridge between goals and accomplishment."
– Jim Rohn

"Discipline is the soul of an army. It makes small numbers formidable; procures success to the weak, and esteem to all."
– George Washington

"Success is not final; failure is not fatal; it is the courage to continue that counts."
– Winston Churchill

What's your plan to close the gap?

That's the first question for you to answer. When you look at the highly productive and successful areas of your life, they all started with a strong plan. Regardless of the subject, the same would apply in every underperforming area of your life.

If you want to break through personal growth barriers, you must start with an *aggressive* plan. This plan must be realistic and challenging, simple but not easy. It needs to cost you something and inspire you as well. It needs to push you forward without breaking you in the process.

When it comes to carrying out change and solving problems—with the goal of serving clients better—one methodology used in many businesses today is lean thinking, communication, and practice. Lean focuses on continuous experimentation and improvement—with fewer resources—while eliminating waste in the process.

This methodology is performed by a series of measurable experiments, observations, and consistent documentation.

Lean thinking helps many business teams *systematize* their approach to continuous improvement in product development, workflows, professional services, and people.

An important extension of lean thinking—used heavily in manufacturing—is PDCA: Plan Do Check Act. Today, this simple approach is at the heart of lean management and, of course, lean thinking. It is used by some of the most respected companies in the world.

My good friend and training partner, Sam Yankelevitch—an expert in lean thinking, instruction, and practice—is a respected LinkedIn Learning Instructor. In one of his sessions, Sam observed the following:

> "PDCA, Plan Do Check Act, acquired a special meaning for the employees. Most of them felt that they were experimenting, and that with each experiment, they were learning something new and applying it to the next. Interestingly, the methodology had provided a sense of psychological safety and helped bring out the best in everyone."

And here's the question for us to ask at this point. If this methodology can help the most respected companies in the world plan, start, and execute better—as they increase service to their clients—can it help you close the gap from where you are today to where you want to be?

I think you would agree. Yes, is the answer.

PLAN

- What is the core problem you need to solve to reduce your gap and reach your goals?

- Is this the right problem for you to work on now?

- What data do you need to fully understand the problem you're having and its root cause?

- Are you likely to solve this?

- What resources do you have, and what other resources are needed to help you?

- What are some possible solutions and specific measures of success?

- How will the results from a few steps translate to a full-scale implementation?

DO

- Start by identifying one problem to solve that will close the gap in your goals.

- What solution are you proposing to reduce the gap?

- Divide this solution into smaller commitments such as "small wins" or goals.

- Start working through your plan while keeping track and recording your observations.

- Evaluate your results after each commitment.

- Apply this approach/solution to other problems affecting your gap and record all observations and results.

- What patterns are developing in each one? Take good notes.

CHECK

- Did your plan work? Study, analyze, and review your results carefully.

- What was highly effective? What was not effective at all?

- If it did, what challenges surfaced in the process?

- What should you eliminate before the next commitment? What else should you eliminate?

- What needs to improve?

- What else needs to improve?

- What did others observe in the process?

- How did your results compare with your success measures?

ACT

- What resources (time, people, materials, technology, etc.) do you need to implement your solution at full scale?

- What additional training (Books, Webinars, Courses, Experience, etc.) do you need to continue moving closer to your goals?

- How can you most accurately measure and track the performance of your process along with your results?

- What opportunities are there now for improvement to reduce the gap even further?

- What have you learned that can be applied to other obstacles in pursuit of your goals or dreams?

- What else have you learned?

What do you need to remove?

Here's where an Executive Coach can serve you exceptionally well. When I signed up for a class to improve my golf game at Miami-Dade College, my professor—after modeling what a real golf swing should look like—would often repeat a short but powerful phrase.

"Too much analysis leads to paralysis."

With one simple phrase, Ms. Garrett helped me to literally remove several obstacles from my mind to center my focus on one synchronized swing.

What I needed most to improve my golf game was not a list of things not to do; it was the reminder to start doing *one concentrated action* after removing everything else from my brain.

Sometimes, you don't make progress when trying to remove the obstacles in your life because you're working too hard to remove all of them simultaneously.

To move forward and realize the life of your dreams, you must start by addressing *one* obstacle at a time and thoroughly understanding *why* it remains a problem.

Coaching will help you become more self-aware of what's getting in the way and walk with you to eliminate your distractions. Once this is accomplished, you'll be able to synchronize your efforts to maximize your concentration and realize the results you desire to reach.

As I work with high-performing clients, I find an interesting pattern that develops. At times, this pattern starts rather quickly, and at other times, it's over a span of a few weeks. What is this pattern? One word describes it well—*decluttering*.

Decluttering, in our context, speaks to a guided process of removing what keeps you from moving through your obstacles to get you from where you are to where you want to be in life.

There are times when this decluttering process is relatively easy to navigate and conquer. And there are other times when deep-seated thinking patterns have created an almost *immovable* mindset about people, methodologies, and situations.

Imagine what you could experience over the next 30-90 days if you intentionally removed the personal obstacles distracting your life and mapped a *new* course of action. Coaching helps facilitate momentum-building discipline to deconstruct recurring obstacles, distractions, and hidden challenges.

Can you infuse extraordinary discipline to overcome recurring obstacles in your life? Can you recover and advance after experiencing life's unexpected storms? Can you face your biggest relational fears with greater confidence and follow through? Yes, you can—with an experienced coach.

You've proven to be a highly disciplined person.

What stops you from committing serious discipline to overcome difficult obstacles and reach your goals?

What feelings does this effort generate? What next steps have you paused?

What obstacles keep getting in the way?

What fears hold you back?

What else holds you back?

What people regularly slow you down or distract you?

What do you need to start?

So, what happens when you start removing one obstacle after another in a way that disempowers their recurring influence over your life? You now have the freedom to *start* moving key areas of your life *forward*. Although some resistance will always be present—that's part of being human—it no longer must control your thinking or your actions.

When my clients experience the freedom that comes from facing their obstacles and working through them in an empowering and collaborative environment, the results are nothing short of transformational.

And here's the best part. Even though their performance in these key areas of their lives has totally missed their undivided focus and capacity, the client is *reinvigorated* with renewed energy to accelerate what matters most in their life. This new focus reminds me of the start of an important race.

"On your mark, get set, go!"

You often hear sports commentators talk about the importance of teams starting well. I enjoy hearing all the statistics about the team who scores first and what you can predict from scoring first and starting well.

You don't have to be on a professional sports team to start well, but you need to start moving your life forward with *purposeful* action to get the desired results. How does coaching help you to start sooner rather than later?

Coaching serves as your partner to *leverage* principles of discipline to not only advance through recurring obstacles but also to make sure you're starting what matters most in your life. The Coaching Advantage can serve as *your* advantage.

I once kept a secret that nobody—not even my parents—knew about. I was terrified to enter deep waters because of my inability to learn how to swim.

My parents signed me up at a place called Small Fry. It was for little dudes like me that required care during the summer when parents worked full-time jobs.

One of the leaders scheduled an activity involving children jumping from the diving board—while trying to catch a ball in mid-air—to score points for their team. I remember the day like it was yesterday.

I knew two things. First, I couldn't swim. That obstacle increased with great intensity. Second, I knew how to catch well. My father played catch with me often. This helped me develop essential catching skills.

So, here's the plan I developed in my brain. Although I can't swim, I can catch the ball in the air. Once I land in the water, I can use the ball as a float and paddle my feet until I reach the shore. Problem solved, right? Wrong!

What I neglected to anticipate fully was the impact of my body and the ball and the water. Once I hit the water, the pressure pushed the ball out of my hands and reach. Houston, we have a problem.

By some miracle, I instinctively began to both panic and paddle like my daughter's rambunctious Corgipoo—Mr. Smokey—until I safely arrived at the tiled pool wall.

Honestly, I didn't think about anything else that day except for getting to the pool wall as fast as possible. I was all alone in my start, execution, and arrival at my destination. Here's the good news.

When you hire an Executive Coach, you never have to swim alone. You can get the support you need to get you from where you are to where you want to be.

We've already established that you're a highly disciplined professional. If that weren't true, you wouldn't have reached this page in my book. I may not be the best writer on the planet, but that really doesn't matter. You've reached this point in the book in part due to your personal discipline.

You already have what's required to start and move forward. You don't have to jump off the diving board and hope that you'll catch the ball. You already have what you need to get to your destination. All you need is an expert coach to call out what remains on pause for you to get started.

Working with an Executive Coach leverages the discipline you've already demonstrated with the capacity for additional discipline waiting to be *evoked* and *practiced*. And this combination is nothing short of transformational to experience.

"Discipline is just choosing between what you want now and what you want most."
– Unknown

"Discipline is the refining fire by which talent becomes ability."
– Roy L. Smith

"Discipline equals freedom."
– Jocko Willink

"The discipline you learn and character you build from setting and achieving a goal can be more valuable than the achievement of the goal itself."
– Bo Bennett

"Successful and unsuccessful people do not vary greatly in their abilities. They vary in their desires to reach their potential."
– John Maxwell

What do you need to execute better to advance through your obstacles?

Let's reiterate what we've established up to this point. First, you walk alongside an experienced coach to *remove* distractions and recurring obstacles—the things that keep getting in the way of your forward progress. Starting is the next step.

You proceed to *implement* a resilient consistency in your daily commitments. This serves to create increasing momentum and unparalleled breakthrough.

Consistency with small commitments today develops into resilient habits tomorrow.

I regularly tell my clients about an important formula to help them realize sustainable change over the course of their lives. This formula is designed to be practiced regularly and intentionally for best results. Let me share with you the principle.

To improve in the areas that matter most in your life, three transformational declarations need to be present and active. These crucial declarations represent a growth mindset.

I call them *The 3 Cs of Transformation*. Each one is essential to your personal and professional development. When synchronized with your goals, they provide you with a clear advantage.

The 3 Cs of Transformation

1. Commitment – I will set clear goals and commit to doing whatever work is required to reach my goals. I will not quit. I choose to persevere through every obstacle I face. I will not make excuses for my lack of performance.

2. Coach – I will invest in coaching. I will commit time, focus, energy, and finances to get better faster. I will be honest about my recurring challenges and what stops me from getting to where I want to be in life.

3. Course of Action – I will be action-oriented in my response to change, even when it's not my preference. I will complete all assigned training. I will make the changes needed to move forward.

Action verses inaction

I started this chapter by highlighting the importance of taking your current level of success and transferring that *same* energy and focus to your current recurring obstacles and challenges.

This is part of the plan to get you from where you are to where you want to be in life. As you know, it won't happen automatically, but it can happen *deliberately*.

I may have rattled you a bit—but surely, I got your attention—when I introduced the word *lazy* into the equation. You accept the fact that you are by no means a *lazy* person, but you're also not giving the same energy to overcome recurring obstacles in at least one key area of your life.

And that is where an experienced coach can make all the difference. We all tend to *avoid* what we don't like. We *procrastinate* dealing with difficult people or situations at work or at home. We *ignore* comments and behaviors.

We might even *pretend* that none of these realities shake us at our core. We communicate as if these things *don't* matter to us. You've acted this way at one time or another and so have I.

Now is not the time for inaction. It's not the time to float in the sea of indecisiveness. It's time to move in the right direction. This requires *action*.

Inaction is common, but not for leaders. Leaders are marked by decisive action, not passive inaction. Action overcomes even the most difficult obstacles. Coaching serves to *facilitate extraordinary discipline*—action. It fuels increasing hope for your future.

Move Forward   Lead Confidently   Accelerate Performance

Consider the five areas below as you consider our thoughts on action versus inaction. Write down one action step per category for you to commit to starting this week. Don't overthink this activity. Be creative about what's possible within your context.

Faith –

Health –

Relationships –

Education –

Work –

Every decision to act—and face your recurring obstacles head-on—is a decision to advance through barriers and move your life forward.

The alternative is to settle for a life that is common and safe. For that reason, be uncommon. Choose action and live courageously.

The Coaching Advantage

Advantage #6

"Executive coaching can help leaders gain clarity, identify blind spots, and develop strategies to overcome obstacles. It is important to find a coach who is a good fit and has experience working with leaders in similar situations. There are several examples of executives who have successfully overcome obstacles with the help of coaching."[18]

---

[18] Stephanie Starling, "How Executive Coaching Can Help You Overcome Career Obstacles," Forbes, February 16, 2021, https://www.forbes.com/sites/stephanieburns/2021/02/16/how-executive-coaching-can-help-you-overcome-career-obstacles/?sh=215b06454e04.

Julian's Coaching Advantage

Julian was in a tough position. His family was settled in a nice beach town. He loved his job and his community. After arriving from vacation, Julian was made aware that he would be fired. This news shocked Julian and his wife.

Stop Being Lazy and Start Moving Forward

As Julian wrestled with this hard reality, he decided to give me a call to invite me into the conversation. He never dreamed of moving on, but it all came crashing down without warning.

Leverage Discipline to Advance Through Your Obstacles

When Julian and I talked, we focused our session on what was ahead, and the discipline required to help him move forward. The decision had been made. There was nothing more for Julian to do but to *move forward*. Sure, this is easier said than done.

What many people—just like Julian—tend to forget is that we often need another voice to help us understand what we can do now—regardless of what's happened to us—and considering all that's currently before us.

Julian took another vacation before making another move. It was just what he needed to reset his perspective on what really matters in life.

Questions for Reflection

1. What recurring obstacles have you avoided but, for one reason or another, continue to surface in key areas of your life?

2. What role has planning played in your recent successes and failures? What lessons have you learned from each outcome?

3. What is the most important thing you can start today to help you triumph over your personal challenges and obstacles?

4. What three gaps are you committed to reducing in your life over the next 90 days?

5. What new milestones do you believe become more attainable when an experienced coach helps you increase personal and professional accountability?

6. When you consider The 3 Cs of Transformation, which of these is your strongest declaration today? Which one is your weakest?

7. What action step—when practiced daily—would indicate to you that you're applying discipline to a key area of your life that lacked this skill?

Chapter 7

Clarify, Evoke, Align, and Focus

Create an Intentional Life Plan to Maximize Your Impact

Exposing Coaching Myths

Myth #8 – Coaching is expensive.

The Real Story

Coaching is highly profitable for the coachee. Imagine being able to dramatically reduce the amount of time it takes you to act on what is highly important in your life. Imagine removing the most critical barriers in your life and creating a plan to move you forward today rather than next year.
The cost of inaction is astounding. Coaching saves you time, energy, and money.

When people read the phrase *"Life Plan,"* they have mixed feelings about the concept and its potential to effect real change in their lives. Some individuals get excited to start talking about this topic and its unexplored possibilities. Others have the opposite reaction.

They don't give it too much attention in part because they've never experienced a *Life Plan Intensive*. As a result, they battle to stay engaged in the conversation.

What about you?

What comes to mind when you read *"Life Plan"*?

As I coach an increasing number of professionals in transition, a few patterns emerge during our conversations. First, the desire to find *meaning* in their work is now at an all-time high.

They're no longer searching exclusively for a larger paycheck. They want to make a difference in their work and further develop their skills. Purpose, impact, and legacy emerge as their renewed focus.

Second, these experienced professionals are highly passionate about finding *alignment* with corporate values and their personal values. If they're unfulfilled in their current position, they start looking internally to see what opportunities better align with their skills, capacity, and goals.

Are you intentional about maximizing the impact you want to have on the lives of those around you?

Some professionals enroll in new certification programs, start a variety of assessments, read books on personal vision, or hire a professional coach. They possess a strong and persistent desire to make a *greater* impact at work, with clients, their communities, and their personal relationships.

But there's another group of professionals—entrepreneurs—determined to leave their corporate jobs and start new business ventures. They're eager to build innovative solutions and solve real-life problems for their clients.

Other entrepreneurs find themselves at a different stage in their lives. They're ready to pursue a new direction for their lives, transition their businesses to new leadership, or sell their business and chart a new course.

Which one of these professional categories best represents where you find yourself today? If you're thinking about your next move or find yourself in the middle of a transition, starting a *Life Plan Intensive* may be just what you need to move you forward.

Life Plan Intensive

What exactly is a *Life Plan Intensive,* and what will it do to give you an advantage as a professional?

A *Life Plan Intensive* (LPI) serves to help you gain a deeper understanding of your life's unique purpose while developing a personalized *Life Plan Profile* (LPP). In this guided four-fold process, you will discover how to move your life forward from where you are to where you want to be.

Clarify   Evoke   Align   Focus

Participating in a *Life Plan Intensive* will give you a distinct professional advantage. It will eliminate clutter and deliver *clarity*. It serves to awaken what has remained hidden or suppressed.

The intensive serves to synchronize your professional and personal life by aligning your values with where you need to go. And to add icing on the cake, it serves to focus your plans, efforts, and concentration in a *singular* direction.

Clarify

When your life has a clear, intentional focus, there's no limit to what impact you can have on those around you. Clarity is the *advantage*.

In this process of transformation, you will develop, assess, and define your personal vision, mission, values, passions, priorities, and responsibilities.

You will gain greater clarity about what's holding you back from finding *more* fulfillment in life. Through a series of proven assessments, you can explore results and explain patterns of thinking, behaviors, and preferences.

Clarify includes defining your personal vision, mission, values, priorities, and responsibilities.

Assessments serve to identify, explore, and validate patterns of thinking while clarifying preferences and strengths.

Next, we identify, assess, and work through the mindsets, challenges, costs, and implications of each challenge emerging from our first module. We then move to establish *Personal Markers* to build upon the previous work and establish clear goals.

What you *measure* gets your *focus*. What gets your focus gets the best of your creativity and energy. Investing time, energy, resources, and focus on clarifying who you are, where you find yourself today, and where you want to be, is a worthwhile investment. It will yield professional and personal dividends for both today and tomorrow.

Why choose to clarify what matters most in your life? It's simple. When you clarify what matters, you can make *better* decisions—by implementing key filters—and discover what motivates you to excel and thrive in life.

What vision—preferred future—have you established for your life?

Describe what it would look like to arrive at your future destination.

What is your mission or purpose in life? What does it lead you to do?

What values serve to consistently influence and direct your thoughts, decisions, plans, and actions?

What are your top daily, weekly, and monthly priorities?

What are your most important responsibilities?

What people, tasks, or activities are you exclusively responsible for?

Why invest so much time, energy, and focus on clarifying what you want your life to look like in the future? Let's get practical. When you have a *target* in life—whether you call it a goal, milestone, or destination—a *shift* takes place in your mind.

Take, for example, a group of six students playing around on the basketball court after school. No one is keeping score, no one establishes any rules, and no one cares about fouls. They're just shooting the ball at the hoop for fun and talking with one another.

But let's suppose that these six students split into two teams of three players each. They decide on a common goal. The first team that scores twenty-one points wins. The players agree on a few basic rules and flip a coin to see which team gets the ball first.

When considering both scenarios, the following observations can be expected to follow. The first group of students will not have high motivation for participating. After throwing the ball around for a while—and if they don't decide to split and play a game against one another—this group will eventually leave the court and return home.

The second group of students will play on high alert. They will study the players on the opposing team carefully. These students will increase their communication with their team members. They will encourage each team member to improve and protect them as best they can.

These students will have uncommon focus, renewed strength, and increasing adrenaline until they *complete* their mission—to win the game.

They won't allow a bad foul to stop them. Why not? Because they're *focused* on the goal—win the game.

Once the students clarified their goal and a few rules of engagement, their intensity and focus launched into a new stratosphere. You can experience *greater* levels of intensity, purpose, and focus when you partner with a coach.

Think about this last month, for example. What was the goal that you wanted to reach by the end of the month? Did your primary focus align with your goal? If you hit your goals, it most likely did align. If you fell short, there was a misalignment somewhere.

What mindset needs to change for you to consistently reach your daily, weekly, monthly, quarterly, and annual goals?

What unexpected challenges did you face last month that somehow derailed your focus?

How did you respond?

Did you plow through them, making the best of things, or did they serve as a more serious obstacle?

Did you outline a clear contingency plan to work around unanticipated problems?

Was there a better way to respond?

How do you know? What needs to be clarified this month before engaging your next obstacle?

Regardless of the potential surprise or change that you may encounter this next month, what mindset is needed today to persevere and reach your goals? Coaching helps you to develop an *anticipatory mindset* to prepare for what's next.

Coaching serves as a catalyst to accelerate leaders and teams from good to great.

Coaching evokes leaders and teams to move from where they are to where they want to be.

Evoke

Once you work through a series of personal assessments and clarifying questions, the next step is to evoke new discoveries, greater self-awareness, and unforeseen possibilities for your future. How exactly do we accomplish this? Through a deliberate sequence of *empowering* questions.

Think of our first phase—Clarify—as the starting point for our adventure. In our second phase—Evoke—we collaborate to dig deeper and unearth buried treasures to bring out the best in you. We drill down into additional implications derived from your initial assessments, reflect from our series of questions, and formulate agreements.

This is not a linear activity. It's an *interactive*, back-and-forth dialogue in its development but highly relevant and practical in its application.

In this second phase, we spend considerable time reflecting, pivoting, and tenaciously shifting your momentum *forward* to where you want to be.

This process will call forth—among other things—strong emotions, persistent obstacles, badgering doubts, relational gaps, unspoken fears, and accepted patterns of thinking.

No coaching session can ever be duplicated. Each is unique and customized for the client—or coachee—because each person is unique. As we seek to evoke from within what matters most in your life, we collaborate through an intentional process of *discovery*.

The following list serves as a basic example of what we cover in this process.

Confirm and Launch

Here we establish the *baseline* for our dialogue. Together, we summarize what's already been clarified. We take additional steps to assess where you are today and where you want to be in key areas of your life. Once this is clearly defined, we launch into the process with greater confidence.

Return, Contextualize, and Reflect

We all have patterns of thinking, disempowering behaviors, and unhealthy habits that sabotage us from reaching our goals. What's often missing from getting back on the right track is understanding what *fueled* these things in the first place.

What held you back from reaching your goal when you first decided to act?

What else held you back?

What did you learn in the process?

What got in the way of your success?

What else got in the way?

What people derailed you in the process?

What events or activities stopped your progress?

What's most important to you right now?

These patterns are best understood as we return to the place where they started. It provides us with the right context to study them further and reflect.

Here we make *observations*—like a persistent reporter—and seek to understand and capture the "lead" of the story. We don't need every single detail, only the most important and relevant details.

Evoke

"To call forth or up: such as to bring to mind or recollection; to re-create imaginatively."[19]

---

[19] "Evoke." Merriam-Webster.com Dictionary, Merriam-Webster, https://www.merriam-webster.com/dictionary/evoke. Accessed 20 Feb. 2023.

Observe, Challenge, and Evoke

Although some of these areas overlap at times, I think you get the point. None of this is linear. Everyone reveals important details about their life's story in their own way. And that's just fine.

The role of the coach is to *organize* what's being spoken, what's not being spoken, noises, bodily expressions, shifts in demeanor, changes in tone of voice, and the selection of specific words being used throughout the dialogue.

I thoroughly enjoy this part. Most of the time, the client is not aware of these sudden shifts or changes in their communication delivery.

So, what does a coach do to help? The coach challenges the client when they discover an *inconsistency* between what the client is saying and what their body is communicating.

The coach points out inconsistencies in the client's *character* by bringing other congruent areas in their lives to the table.

And here is where the coach digs deeper to call forth what's really going on in the mind and heart of the client. It's like peeling an onion one layer at a time. You want to get to the core issue. To do so, you must remove one layer at a time.

What got in the way when you started?
What's getting in the way now?
What stopped you in the past?
What's stopping you right now?
What caused your tone to change?
What made you lower your head?
What's the *reason* for your inconsistent behavior?

Understand the Story

As an extension of the observation process, the coach pursues a good understanding of the story of the client. Again, not every detail is required. Only those details that serve the purpose of learning what's *impacting* the client right now are of significance.

Challenge the Narrative

I learn helpful information about the client as they talk through different challenges and obstacles. Often, a disqualifying narrative—one that keeps them stuck—surfaces. The client not only believes this false narrative but also tells others about it.

The client has chosen to *believe* their own story and inability to make forward progress. This narrative, if entertained, is detrimental to their success. Therefore, we must challenge the narrative.

Don't beat yourself up over this common narrative. All of us—you and I included—create *debilitating* narratives at one time or another.

Thankfully, our second phase—Evoke—gives you the tools to work through these narratives. Here are some common questions to start peeling back the layers of disempowerment.

What first led you to believe this statement?
What were you hoping that it would accomplish?
What's not true about this now?
What lack of progress surprised you the most?
What is the reason to continue thinking this way?
What would happen if you changed the story?

What has believing in this story truly produced?
What's most difficult for you to face now?
What's really holding you back? What else?
What makes it difficult to change your mind?
What stops you from moving forward now?

Shift and Flip the Script

For those of us who wear eyeglasses throughout the day, there's always the possibility of dropping your eyeglasses and breaking them. Although not as dramatic, the reality of scratching your lens is likely more probable. I speak from experience here.

In both examples, buying a new pair of eyeglasses is certainly a good option. Here's the principle: If you can't fix it, *change* it.

When it comes to the application point in the coaching process, there are times when *flipping* the script is the right move to help you see things from a different perspective.

You've bought into a story of your own making, but now it's time for you to change the next chapter.

How do you do this? You start by shifting your perspective—or mindset—and flipping the script of your narrative. To be more dramatic, you can tear up the script you wrote initially and start writing a *new* script to believe and follow.

You are the director in this new narrative. As the coaching process develops over each session, you gain greater *confidence* to write this new script, act decisively, and start realizing your dreams.

Let's not get too far too fast, at least not yet. For now, we're walking you through a process of change. And change, by its very nature, takes some time to decide, process, and act upon. And this leads us to our next step in the evoking process.

Structure Thematically: Identify, Validate, and Chart Themes

At this point, we celebrate the progress made together as we look ahead to what's truly possible for you to achieve. Together, we start our next course of action by formulating a *structure* to support our discoveries.

It's one thing to talk about themes, progress, and possibilities and another thing altogether to see it unfold right before your eyes.

I'm a visual guy. I think this thematic structuring helps me to see themes, patterns, possibilities, and more just as much as it helps my clients.

We begin this next step by highlighting past, present, and future *themes*—consisting of no more than seven key areas—using three evolving themes: primary, secondary, and tertiary.

As we list each area, we're identifying, validating data, and charting our themes for each one. For example, if the first area we identify is relationships, we would identify and validate primary, secondary, and tertiary themes of the past—historical realities, today—what's happening now and in the future.

Next, we measure *progress*. We identify, validate, and document or chart key obstacles, significant advances, and key wins and losses.

Lastly, we identify, validate, and document or chart future possibilities in each of the three areas. This is the fun part, although, at times, it can stretch clients way beyond their comfort zones.

And once these key factors are documented, we are ready to chart a *new course* after taking the time to interpret and apply what we're learning together in the process.

Key Area: Relationships

Themes:	Primary	Secondary	Tertiary
1. Past			
2. Present			
3. Validate			
4. Chart			

Progress:	Obstacles	Advances	Wins/Losses
1. Past			
2. Present			
3. Validate			
4. Chart			

Possibilities:	Primary	Secondary	Tertiary
1. Present			
2. Future			
3. Validate			
4. Chart			

Interpret and Apply

In the world of theology and hermeneutics, there's a simple framework used to study a passage from scripture: Observation, Interpretation, and Application. This progressive approach has been used by Professors and Pastors worldwide.

One purpose behind this methodology is to establish *consistent* and *reliable* patterns of biblical interpretation and application.

I follow this same pattern as I work with professionals on developing a Life Plan. I spend hours observing, asking questions, and noting curious patterns of behavior. In theological circles, good observation leads to good interpretation.

You never want to jump to conclusions too fast. On the contrary, facilitating a *Life Plan Intensive* is not accomplished in only a few hours. It can take days or even weeks to unpack, but what's produced is immeasurable and *priceless*.

Interpretation has to do with communicating what your observations and discoveries have produced. It's the product of your investigation. As we explained in the previous section, this is where you can chart a new course for your future and open new possibilities for what's ahead.

Here's another important factor to consider. The better job a coach does with his or her interpretation—in collaboration with the client—the better and more concise the application will be.

As you partner with an experienced coach, you too will discover and see how good interpretation leads you to good application and practice.

Align

Now we arrive at the third phase—Align—of our *Life Plan Intensive*. Together, we've clarified and defined, validated, and charted. We've worked through the disappointments, the missed opportunities, and our responsibility in each one.

We have the information we need to move in the desired direction, but what specific direction is there to consider? For starters, this goes back to where you want to be—your *destination*.

We evoke the best from within you to produce the best through you by first aligning your direction with your desired destination.

Why is it so important to align your efforts with your desired destination? There are many reasons, but here are several to consider.

You reduce your stress levels due to a lack of misaligned work.

Your work is more purposeful and directional. Maximizing your time—partly by eliminating waste—is a byproduct of this third phase.

You develop greater motivation to envision what's possible and create a concrete plan of action to get you there.

You design a realistic but challenging *framework* to maintain your values, personal vision, and focus. You gain greater satisfaction in life by aligning your passion with your work.

As we work through each key area together, the goal in this section is to align plans, efforts, energy, resources, and more with where you want to be in the future.

When there's alignment, many other factors are eliminated from the equation. To deliberately align with your future destination is not optional but *essential* to your long-term success.

The following framework represents a simplified version of this entire process.

Consider and Envision New Possibilities

Key Area: Relationships

Destination: Build Existing Relationships at work

A New Framework and Direction

1. What's the destination?
2. Why does it matter now?
3. What makes it a non-negotiable?
4. What new possibilities exist?
5. What timeline do these new possibilities have before they're gone and no longer available?
6. What gaps need to be prioritized and closed as soon as possible to guarantee long-term success?
7. What's the best course of action to follow?
8. What additional support is needed?
9. Chart the plan and the progress (30-60-90 days)
10. What other adjustments are needed to maximize alignment with future possibilities and goals?

Move Forward   Lead Confidently   Accelerate Performance

Focus

At last, we've arrived at the fourth phase—Focus—of our *Life Plan Intensive*. Although this chapter only represents a summary of what to expect, I know the concept is much easier to understand. The *Life Plan Intensive* journey is always intentional, never linear, and increasingly satisfying.

Clarify   Evoke   Align   Focus

When we define this last phase with the word *focus*, what exactly do we mean by this? Focus has to do with getting to your destination *faster*. That's the heart of this last phase. When you run in a race, you typically remove all unnecessary weight from your body. Removing your favorite watch is not an issue if you know it can make the *difference* between winning the race or coming in second place.

To get you from where you are to where you want to be in the key areas of your life is not for the weary. Here are some of the action steps I lead you through to hyper-focus on getting to your goals as fast as possible.

Develop an aggressive plan of action.
Leave nothing to "chance" but take bold steps.
Plan for what's difficult, not for what's easy.
Make each day count and count each day.
Sharpen the focus of your mind.
Get on an ambitious action-focused schedule.
Act decisively, not passively.
Measure progress and adjust quickly to changes.
Clarify what matters and remove what doesn't.

Stay aligned with the next step to your destination.
Establish coaching and learning milestones.
Develop a progressive list of lessons learned.
Reduce the noise and the clutter in your life.
Concentrate more on what you do best.
Delegate tasks to others to support your focus.
Become more self-aware of your development.
And here are several others: Design a sustainable life plan that builds healthy rhythms and increases your productivity. Explore, reduce, and align career options with your purpose, plans, and goals.
Leverage training, skills, talents, and abilities to be your best self.

Imagine what you could achieve if the biggest obstacle holding you back were suddenly removed?

Although highly simplified, I hope this gives you a comprehensive overview of the entire process. If you would like to be coached through a *Life Plan Intensive*, several meeting options are available these days to better serve you.

But I do have to warn you, participating in a *Life Plan Intensive* will lead you to realize The Coaching Advantage in your life. It has the potential to *dramatically* change your life and the lives of those around you.

Clarify   Evoke   Align   Focus

The Coaching Advantage

Advantage #7

"Coaching can help individuals, including leaders, develop effective life plans. Coaching can help individuals identify their goals and values, create a plan to achieve those goals, and hold themselves accountable for making progress. It is important to regularly reassess one's plan to ensure it aligns with one's current priorities and values. Many successful leaders have used coaching to develop effective life plans."[20]

---

[20] Rachel Dalton, "How life coaching can help you develop a better life plan," Fast Company, January 11, 2021, https://www.fastcompany.com/90592305/how-life-coaching-can-help-you-develop-a-better-life-plan.

Carey's Coaching Advantage

Carey had more potential for greatness than she could gather on her own. After her parents divorced, it was difficult for Carey to get motivated about anything significant. Although Carey had many mentors, she consistently perceived herself as regularly falling short on opportunities.

Carey worked long hours and left dissatisfied after every shift. She was very good at her job and learned how to become highly efficient at whatever was asked of her. But deep down inside Carey, she was bored, unchallenged, and *ready* to consider something different.

Create an Intentional Life Plan to Maximize Your Impact

When Carey and I met for our initial coaching session, she quickly shared the desire to find something else with *greater* meaning and purpose.

The problem was that Carey had zero plans in place to find anything. It was more like a gesture of hope than a burning ambition.

This series of coaching sessions were quite interesting to me. Most of my clients are highly ambitious, ready to climb Mount Everest, or highly educated. Carey was none of the above.

Carey realized that there was something brewing inside her to make a change, but she had no idea how to *start* this process or what questions to ask. She need not worry. That was my job!

Brainstorming can be helpful, but in Carey's case, that's all she did. She regularly added dreaming to this exercise. None of it was helpful.

As we worked through our sessions, I came to understand a key factor about Carey. Although she did not want to invest the energy required to move herself forward in life, her dissatisfaction with work was starting to override her lack of drive.

Clarify, Evoke, Align, and Focus

Brainstorming created too many options for Carey. This self-awareness on Carey's part helped her to narrow down her focus. As we began to regularly reduce the available options, it led to times of deeper reflection and consideration of what was now possible for her to start.

Carey started making healthy connections as our coaching sessions progressed. She became aware of the importance of getting certified to become useful for prospective employers. She took steps to improve her health and quality of life.

But the one realization that likely served as the catalyst for every step forward was the realization that your past *never* has to define your future. Could you blame Carey for having a low sense of self-esteem? No, not really.

As with many young professionals, Carey had to *believe* in her potential to get what she wanted as she followed a good plan to get her from where she was to where she wanted to be. And this is where an experienced coach can help you to *align* your life with your values to arrive at your destination.

Questions for Reflection

1. What would you say are the top 5-7 areas in your life that need to move forward and get better faster?

2. What would be the most helpful area to explore with the goal of gaining greater clarity?

3. What would be the most helpful area to explore with the goal of gaining greater awareness by evoking new possibilities for your future?

4. What key areas would you say need immediate alignment with your desired destination and goals?

5. Although uncharacteristic of you, which key areas require greater focus and deliberate concentration?

6. What's the core issue holding you back from getting from where you are to where you want to be?

7. Are you ready to move forward, lead better, and realize the life of your dreams?

Chapter 8

Stop Dreaming and Get to Work

Start Your Next Visionary Adventure With One Step

Exposing Coaching Myths

Myth #9 – Coaching is a one-size-fits-all approach.

The Real Story

Coaching is unique to each person because each person is unique. **Coaching is immeasurably personalized and contextualized to the present reality of the coachee.**

Coaching focuses exclusively on you and on the challenges you bring to the session. Coaching starts with curiosity and ends with time-bound action steps.

One of the most exciting parts of my coaching practice is the opportunity to meet with amazing visionaries from around the globe. Listening closely to these visionaries as they verbally paint their dreams on the canvas of possibilities is inspiring.

These visionaries don't think like other people think. They look far *beyond* the limitations of today to what's *possible* to accomplish tomorrow. They're so forward-thinking in their approach to life that they stimulate others to envision a new future.

Some professionals today visualize and envision what's possible for their future business or career over a span of weeks, months, and even years. They park on the canvas of possibilities during times of reflection and planning, but unfortunately, they *never* move beyond that point.

This apparent roadblock can develop increasing levels of dissatisfaction and frustration at work. It may spark some level of hope and excitement within their soul, but this doesn't last very long.

You have dreams and visions of what could be and should be for your future. But that's not enough. You need much more than a great vision to effect change.

As I coach energetic and visionary professionals, I often hear them make comments such as the following:

"I can see a new approach to this business, one that can help our clients grow exponentially."

"If we build a global network of leaders, we can accelerate our mission in unprecedented ways."

"We will make sacrifices now to gain more experience. This will help us support our plans to build a better school in the future."

"We will move our office to Miami to better serve our international clients and streamline our business operations."

"By making this one change, we will be able to develop more leaders faster and prepare the next generation for future growth opportunities."

"Through this innovation, our business would realize the potential to scale without limits and without hiring excessive support staff."

Let's close the loop to address what our chapter title and subtitle have left open. How do you stop dreaming and get to work?

What's the one step that helps you start your next visionary adventure? **Action** is the step. It's the way you get to work to start realizing your dreams and begin your next visionary adventure.

"The 2-step process for exceptional results:
(1) Spend a little time each day thinking about the highest leverage activity available to you.
(2) Spend a little time each day working on it."
– James Clear

"One day you will wake up and there won't be any more time to do the things you've always wanted.
Do it now."
– Novelist Paulo Coelho

Results *don't* automatically appear. There's no magic potion to drive you forward in life and accelerate your performance. Decisive action is what *precedes* results. Without it, results are only a wish. Don't build your life or your team on a wish.

Build your dreams and accomplish your goals with purposeful action. Action is really at the heart of effective coaching. Coaching is not designed around making you feel better about yourself. It's neither therapy nor a session to vent all your problems and frustrations.

Coaching is so much more than these things. And by the way, it is action-focused and action-driven. Coaching is all about walking with you in a collaborative partnership to take the next *action step* in your life. Coaching involves making forward progress in the areas that matter most in your life.

Let's dig deeper into some of the benefits of coaching you can expect to receive as they relate to forward movement—action. Together, we'll take a closer look at several factors involved in this action-oriented journey.

> "Your beliefs become your thoughts,
> Your thoughts become your words,
> Your words become your actions,
> Your actions become your habits,
> Your habits become your values,
> Your values become your destiny."
> — Mahatma Gandhi

Let's get to work!

Destination

Getting to work on your next visionary adventure begins with *defining* your objective and desired destination. Don't limit yourself by only dreaming about where you want to be in the future. Write it down on a whiteboard, post it on social media, and add it to your favorite mobile reminder app.

What are the fundamental qualities of your destination? What do you really want?

What other characteristics are you envisioning?

What would defining your next visionary adventure look like in only a few sentences?

What would it mean to arrive at your destination?

What are you expecting to feel once you arrive?

Determination and Commitment

Focus is powerful, and so is decisiveness. As you've already noticed, realizing your dreams and what you want most in life require uncommon clarity. When the clarity of your destination is defined, resolute determination and commitment is sure to follow.

Determination consists of doing *whatever* is needed to arrive at your destination. It means not allowing challenges or obstacles to derail you on your journey. Commitment is the promise to follow through and *finish* what you've started. It means that devotion, perseverance, steadfastness, and loyalty to the destination have been engrained into your character.

There are a few *determinations*—which some call resolutions—that should remain at the forefront of your thinking at this point in the process. To reach your destination or goal, internal tenacity is required. As you will observe, although there can be many others, let's start with the basics.

I will do everything within my power to reach my goal—the destination.

I will get the coaching I need to get me from where I am to where I want to be.

I will not make excuses, but I will follow through on every commitment I make toward my goal.

I will not be passive but proactive when challenges surface that need to be addressed.

I will take the initiative to get work done rather than procrastinate.

I will not be casual about what activities are required but highly intentional and action-oriented.

I will not allow circumstances to distract me, but I'm determined to remain focused on my plan.

I will make whatever sacrifices are required to accelerate progress toward the goal.

I will not waste time, but I will maximize every moment to do more in less time.

I will not waste money, but I will leverage every dollar to invest wisely.

I will not sacrifice relationships, but I will prioritize loving people and serving their needs.

I will measure my progress and make whatever adjustments are needed to stay on track.

I am highly determined and wholly committed to reaching my goal.

"Take the first step in faith. You don't have to see the whole staircase, just take the first step."
– Martin Luther King Jr.

"Success seems to be connected with action. Successful people keep moving. They make mistakes, but they don't quit."
– Conrad Hilton

"Action may not always bring happiness, but there is no happiness without action."
– Benjamin Disraeli

"The only way to change your life is to take action today. Not tomorrow, not next week, but today."
– Unknown

Course of Action

You've established a clear destination. You've articulated where you're going and what singular and focused determination is required to get you there. Now you're ready to start building the course of action, the plan, to arrive at your destination.

How do you do this? You start by mapping a trail from your destination back to where you are today. Next, you ask the question, "What steps are required to get to where I need to be. The steps *required* serve as your course of action.

There are many steps involved—and seldom linear—to arrive at your destination. Here's a list of questions that help to determine what next steps may be required in your situation.

What online course, certification, intensive, or other training program do I need to complete?

What software or app do I need to purchase to maximize my time and stay highly organized?

What experiences do I still lack?

What people do I need to serve on my team?

What will I need them to do?

What investments of time, talent, and resources will I need to dedicate to reach my goals?

What mindset do I need to adopt to develop greater resiliency, focus, and action?

What contingency plans do I need to establish when things don't work out as planned?

Who will serve as my coach to make sure I stay accountable to my plans and deliver results?

What milestones do I need to establish to objectively measure my performance?

Timeline

Once you have a solid course of action in place, establishing specific timelines for each step required will significantly increase your probability of success throughout your journey. A timeline provides you with the *framework* for success.

Having a clear timeline, one detailing clear milestones, objectives, due dates, deliverables, and other key factors, is essential.

What does a timeline do for your short-term and long-term goals? For starters, having a timeline is another step forward in leading you to *act* rather than keep dreaming for another few months.

I find that busy business professionals dream of doing more and realizing the life of their dreams, but they're not always tuned in to how to stay accountable throughout the process.

Here's where coaching serves you exceptionally well by keeping you on plan and moving forward, one milestone at a time.

A timeline will apply a generous amount of pressure and motivation to your course of action. It will strengthen your resolve, eliminate common distractions, and keep you focused on the right activities.

A simplified approach to what I'm talking about would look something like this example below for a business leader wanting to write their first book.

Milestone #1

Complete Table of Contents

Milestone Ownership

The author will be responsible for the entirety of this assignment.

Objectives

To complete the first draft of the Table of Contents for review with your book coach.

Soft Deadline: March 1st

Hard Deadline: March 15th

Deliverables and Key Factors

Complete the first draft of the Table of Contents with subtitles, using strong action verbs and relevant sentence structure for business executives.

The author should provide three colleagues with copies of the Table of Contents for review and constructive feedback.

The author should evaluate their selection of words and phrases to make sure they stimulate vision, possibilities, and hope for the reader.

Initiative

Here's where "the rubber meets the road" by moving from the envisioning and planning phase to the action and activities phase. It's time to start!

This reminds me of a conversation with a group of engineers from Germany. They spoke extensively about the importance of investing 80% of your time in planning and 20% in execution.

Struck by this apparent imbalance—and having a bias for action—I asked for further explanation. They told me that the biggest problem we have these days is spending too little time planning and too much time fixing our mistakes down the line because of poor planning.

Initiative and execution are productive only when preceded by aggressive analysis and rigorous planning. Without them, your momentum can quickly get derailed.

However, when planning was thorough and anticipatory, it would make the execution of any project smoother and with fewer mistakes. This team was one of the best groups of engineers in the world. I'll never forget their advice.

Now, back to our topic. So, once you've invested the time required to carefully plan your course of action and establish strong timelines, action is what follows. Don't procrastinate at this point in your adventure. *Start* now. Here is where the magic begins. On your mark, get set, go!

Activities

Activities should always drive results, especially as they relate to advancing through your course of action. If the activities you've planned don't move you forward *toward* your goals, they're a waste of time. Initiatives and activities without a clearly defined purpose are useless.

Make sure that your activities are keeping you centered and aligned with where you need to go next. Here's where hiring a professional coach can help you save major time, energy, and resources.

Coaches help you to align with the best plans and refocus your energy. They help you to stay on track when everything around you seeks to derail you and move your momentum off course.

Potential Obstacles

If you haven't faced major obstacles, it's only a matter of time before you do. Coaches help you anticipate and plan for potential obstacles ahead of their arrival.

Why does this even matter? Obstacles—when met without proper preparation—can totally *sabotage* whatever progress you've made on your timeline. This is why it's so important to anticipate and prepare for their arrival.

Once again, here is where your propensity to be action-focused can serve to derail obstacles and challenges before they catch you by surprise. This is how you get to work on securing the destination of your adventure. Work it and keep moving forward.

Opportunities

I can recall when I worked as a Major Accounts Manager for the largest logistics company in the world. It was one of the most challenging jobs in the company. I was tasked to hunt the largest accounts in the district that currently had our fierce competitor as their main source of transportation.

I was highly motivated to be the best in my district. Not only did I want to perform at my best, but I also determined to solve highly complex logistical challenges for my clients.

I recall my tenacity in those days to spend as much time as possible with my clients and dig for an integrated approach to solving their greatest needs.

What I discovered was that I thoroughly enjoyed coordinating meetings with partners, drafting good proposals, and realizing a win-win for both my clients and our company. In the process, I was able to establish meaningful relationships with each of my clients.

This approach to reaching my professional goals through developing relevant solutions and strong relationships served as a proven template for other key endeavors.

The more I implemented this template with my clients, the more opportunities I was able to capture. Part of this involved a disposition to stop dreaming and get to work. And this work came in the form of *consistent* planning and action.

After serious planning, action is the next step that helps you to start your next visionary adventure and open new doors of opportunity.

The Coaching Advantage

Advantage #8

"Coaching can help individuals, including leaders, achieve goals that may have previously seemed unattainable. Coaching can provide individuals with accountability, motivation, and support as they work toward their goals. Successful leaders have used coaching to achieve great results, such as improving their productivity or advancing their careers. Coaching can be a valuable tool for anyone looking to make significant progress toward their goals."[21]

---

[21] Jolie Pollak, "How Coaching Can Help You Reach Goals That Seemed Unattainable," The New York Times, February 23, 2021,

Cesar's Coaching Advantage

When Cesar and I met for one of our coaching sessions, the decision had been brewing for quite some time. After contemplating ending the relationship with his business partner, Cesar was ready to act and move on with the next chapter of his business and his life.

There comes a time when you must *stop* dreaming about the future and *start* acting on what you want and where you want to be. There's a time to take the first step. There's a time to shift your focus and momentum forward.

Start Your Next Visionary Adventure with One Step

This is how coaching shines brightly. It keeps you honest about your *real* progress, not your *perceived* progress. Cesar was treading in his partnership, and he knew it. Coaching served to help Cesar start swimming laps around the pool.

Cesar discovered a hard truth. No matter how hard you try to change your business partner, you can't change them. They must *want* to change for change to become a reality in their lives.

Cesar realized that he was the one that needed to make the next move. It was time for him to align his dreams with a *new* set of plans. What next step is required to move you from dreaming to adventure?

---

https://www.nytimes.com/2021/02/23/smarter-living/coaching-unattainable-goals.html.

Move Forward   Lead Confidently   Accelerate Performance

Questions for Reflection

1. When you stop to reflect on clearly defining the objectives for your goals and/or destination, what's easy for you to define? What's more difficult to define?

2. What would others say about your commitment and determination to work through difficult challenges and reach your end goals?

3. What do you find difficult about setting a course of action to reach your desired destination? Explain your answer.

4. What type of timeline motivates you to follow what it demands of you? What's your track record with successfully reaching your past timelines?

5. Do others often comment positively on the congruence you have with initiative and activities or the lack of its presence in your pursuits?

6. What recurring obstacles continue to derail you from advancing to your goals and/or destination?

7. What new opportunities have you been made aware of that would be a good fit to move you forward in pursuit of your destination?

Chapter 9

Get Better Faster

Increase Your Performance with Hybrid Coaching and Training

Exposing Coaching Myths

Myth #10 – Coaching is a quick fix.

The Real Story

Coaching is a process, not a gimmick. It takes time to work through significant relational challenges, personal obstacles, problems at work, a lack of direction, and so many other life-related difficulties.

The process of coaching may be slow on the surface, but the impact of coaching moves deep and wide to stimulate action.

Transitions are difficult for most of us. I recall one manager I reported to who was totally unaware of the transition taking place in the company and in the people under his leadership.

The company was growing at an accelerated pace. The managers and supervisors around him were also developing their skills and growing rapidly. But the problem was that this leader of leaders was *not* growing.

Unfortunately, he remained stuck in the old dictatorial ways of managing and leading people. He leveraged the fear of being fired as his primary weapon of mass economic destruction for your life if you refused to align with his extreme demands.

His approach was to intimidate you beyond your capacity to think about any other option but full submission to his every word. Eventually, this leader lost his cool with his regional boss during a talk.

He was directed to go home and "cool off" for a time. From that point forward, there was an obvious shift in his entire approach to leading people.

Coaching Increases Performance

To increase effectiveness as a leader—while developing your people—get coaching, grow your coaching skills, and develop your soft skills. If you don't, you're guaranteed to become *irrelevant* to the people you lead and the clients you manage.

In today's fast-paced world, if you don't shift to a coaching approach to lead your people, you will find disengagement, low morale, and staff turnover increasing like an aggressive form of cancer. People have *changed*, and so have you. You must stay *ahead* of this change to lead effectively.

The idea behind *get better faster* is not exclusively for your people; it's for your benefit as well. Gaining a competitive advantage in today's business world involves training your people to perform at their very best, but it also means training *yourself* with even greater intensity and commitment.

Several studies support the positive impact of coaching on individual and team performance. These studies are not limited to a select group of industries. Some of the highlights uncovered from these studies are very impressive.

An astounding study by the International Coach Federation found that organizations experienced a return on investment (ROI) of between 7 and 8 times the cost of coaching.[22] That's too big of a return to ignore. There's an investment to consider, but the dividends far exceed your investment.

---

[22] International Coach Federation (ICF), ICF Global Coaching Client Study (Lexington, KY: International Coach Federation, 2009)

A meta-analysis of coaching studies conducted by the University of Texas found that coaching improved work performance by an average of 22%.[23] Employees respond better when they know what to do, why it matters, and who they can count on when they need further direction or face unexpected challenges.

A study by Manchester Inc. found that coaching significantly improved goal attainment, job satisfaction, and reduced stress.[24] Do these factors positively impact performance? You bet it does! What impact would you realize by exceeding your team's goals by 20% to 30% have on your bottom line? How would it serve your clients?

The favorable impact of coaching on employee performance in Pakistan's banking sector found that coaching had a strong effect on increasing employee productivity.[25]

Finally, a study by the American Management Association found that coaching led to improved communication, teamwork, and leadership skills.[26] This pattern of increasing performance is *not* accidental but intentional and expected.

---

[23] Richard J. Jones, Stephanie A. Woods, and Yves R. F. Guillaume, "The effectiveness of workplace coaching: A meta-analysis of learning and performance outcomes from coaching," Journal of Occupational and Organizational Psychology 88, no. 2 (2015)

[24] Manchester Inc., "Building a coaching culture: Key strategies for embedding coaching skills and practices into your organization" (2001).

[25] Muhammad Jahanzeb Khan and Sami Farooq, "The impact of coaching on employee performance: Evidence from the banking sector of Pakistan," International Journal of Training and Development 25, no. 1 (2021): 71-87.

[26] American Management Association, "Coaching: A global study of successful practices," accessed March 3, 2023, https://www.amanet.org/articles/coaching-a-global-study-of-successful-practices/.

These studies demonstrate the impact coaching can have on executive performance, team performance, and employee performance while highlighting its value as a *strategic* development tool to increase productivity and profitability.

> **"Coaching is seen as one way for organizations to broaden access to leadership development. It goes back to what you're trying to do. You're trying to personalize experiences. You're trying to engage employees. Both of those things can be done with coaching."[27]**

When asked about the impact of coaching, "Marcel, why are you so *passionate* about coaching," my response is quite plain. I have personally seen how coaching has *dramatically* transformed individuals, couples, teams, and businesses—both small and large—along with other organizations.

Coaching serves to unify teams and increase employee engagement. It truly serves as a catalyst.

And if coaching has transformed other leaders and their teams, it can absolutely change you and your teams as well. Coaching can lead you and your people from where you *are* to where you want to *be*.

---

[27] Torch. "Leveraging Coaching," 6.

Aggressively Reduce the Skills Gap

But there's something unexpected and altogether inspirational when you *leverage* the power of executive coaching with soft skills training and coach skills training. What is it? It's the parallel development of professional competency *and* action-driven resilience.

In the process, the skills gap gets *reduced*. We already know that the skills gap is expanding faster than companies can presently manage. With increasing turnover and mounting pressure to do more work with fewer people, skills training often gets set aside for future consideration. Shortfalls in performance and operational efficiency eventually surface and deliver profit-shattering results to businesses of all shapes and sizes.

As C-level executives in the *Closing the Skills Gap 2023* Wiley University Services survey responded to the question: "Do you believe there is a gap in the skills your organization needs and what your employees possess right now?" 69% of these leaders marked yes as their answer.[28]

This stunning percentage is anything but insignificant. It speaks to a serious skills deficit that must be addressed immediately. How would you have responded? Would other executive leaders on your team agree or disagree? How will you assess the need to close the skills gap with your people?

---

[28] Capranos, D., Magda, A. J. (2023). Closing the skills gap 2023: Employer perspectives on educating the post-pandemic workforce. Maitland, FL: Wiley Inc.

Four Synergistic Methodologies

As I meet with business owners and executive leaders, they often talk about the growing skills gap with their people and what can be done to solve them. They're frustrated but not alone. As research clearly shows, multiple industries are wrestling with this very same problem.

Identifying what skills need to be trained or retrained is not the problem. Finding the *best* methodology to drive deeper engagement and extraordinary results is a great mystery to solve.

How do you train your people while increasing employee engagement? How do you equip your managers to develop their skills at a *sustainable* pace?

How do you train your leaders and guarantee that these skills will be implemented within the next month and beyond? Establishing a *Hybrid Culture of Coaching and Training—HCCT*—is the answer. This is how you change your culture from good to great.

As one executive leader affirms, "It appears that organizations may be using more traditional training to teach the skills and then methods such as coaching to ensure these new skills are truly infused into participants' daily work lives."[29]

Creating an effective culture of coaching and training is possible. It requires extreme ownership, action, financial investments, and a commitment to the process by executive leadership. Once that's clear, we can get to work right away.

---

[29] Torch. "Leveraging Coaching," 6.

What is a Hybrid Culture of Coaching and Training, HCCT?

HCCT is an innovative leadership skills development program designed to accelerate performance and increase engagement with executive leaders, teams, and employees.

It creates a robust culture of coaching that empowers leaders to develop future leaders faster.

We accomplish this by blending four synergistic methods—delivered weekly, bi-weekly, and monthly.

1. Soft Skills Training
2. Coach Skills Training
3. On-Demand Training
4. Executive Coaching

1. Soft Skills Training

Soft skills are personal qualities that enable you to communicate well with other people.[30] They serve to build relational bridges, develop essential people skills, and increase performance. Soft skills training is delivered in-person and, at times, online.

As a business leader, soft skills serve to integrate business intelligence with relational principles. These skills tend to overlap in many professional environments, creating exceptional synergies and possibilities for growth. If you want to have a greater impact on your teams, you must work to radically sharpen your soft skills.

As a high-performing, ambitious, and people-centric leader, to move forward, lead confidently, and accelerate performance, soft skills training is vital to your leadership development.

Once you get on board and start improving, your commitment to continuous learning and development will motivate your executive leaders and serve as a great model for their teams. To grow your people, you *first* must grow yourself.

You can't lead your people to reach exceptional performance if you aren't growing and performing at the highest levels of professional excellence.

---

[30] "Soft Skills," Oxford Learner's Dictionaries, accessed March 6, 2023, https://www.oxfordlearnersdictionaries.com/us/definition/english/soft-skills?q=soft+skills.

"There is a broad realization that great leaders, mentors, and coaches help companies achieve better performance. Great leadership is a business imperative. It's a value proposition. It drives financial outcomes and provides organizations with a strategic edge in the talent marketplace."

– Ajit Chouhan, Senior Director of Human Resources, Hewlett Packard Enterprise[31]

---

[31] Torch. "Leveraging Coaching and Mentoring to Create More Effective Leaders." Harvard Business Review, January 2023, accessed March 3, 2023, https://torch.io/wp-content/uploads/2023/01/Leveraging-Coaching-and-Mentoring-to-Create-More-Effective-Leaders_Torch_HBRAS.pdf.

I think you get the point. You *can't* lead your people down a road that you yourself have *not* walked. My recommendation for soft skills training is one-to-two days of training per month.

Although some companies prefer live online training via ZOOM or TEAMS, most *interactive* training is performed in person. Below is a sample list of today's most popular soft skills.

Emotional Intelligence	Adaptability to Change
Collaboration	Critical Thinking
Problem-Solving	Conflict Resolution
Tenacious Character	Work Ethic
Leadership	Time Maximization
Interpersonal Skills	Teamwork
Creativity	Innovation
Written Communication	Speaking Confidently
Presentations Skills	Diversity and Culture
Positive Attitude	Being Goal-Oriented
Sales and Negotiation	Tenacious Character
Business Networking	Leading Virtually
Building Relationships	Developing Trust
Accountability	Delegation
Effective Feedback	Coaching and Mentoring
Active Listening	Evoking Awareness
Customer Service	Value and Respect
Developing People	Leading Teams
Decision-Making	Extreme Ownership
Continuous Learning	Managing Stress
Planning and Execution	Work-Life Balance
Self-Management	Extraordinary Discipline
Strategic Thinking	Event Planning

2. Coach Skills Training

Creating a culture of coaching to drive long-term results requires effective and intentional coach skills training. It starts with a clear understanding of what coaching *is* and is *not*.

Coaching is not mentoring.
Coaching is not teaching.
Coaching is not counseling.
Coaching is not therapy.
Coaching is not recreation.
Coaching is not manipulation.
Coaching is not motivation, although it does motivate professionals to act decisively.

The International Coaching Federation (ICF) defines coaching as "partnering with clients in a thought-provoking and creative process that inspires them to maximize their personal and professional potential. The process of coaching often unlocks previously untapped sources of imagination, productivity, and leadership."[32]

Executive leaders and managers need to develop *effective* tools to lead, equip, and empower their people. Coaching skills are exactly what they need to learn to deliver *consistent* results while developing their people in the process.

---

[32] "What is Coaching?" International Coaching Federation, ICF.org, December 21, 2021, https://coachingfederation.org/about

The reason for this is clear. Creating a culture of coaching *enhances* a culture of learning. Coach skills training serves to build the tools and the momentum required for your leaders to realize sustainable performance growth.

Coach skills training is delivered primarily online—through one-hour coach skills training sessions—but it can be delivered in person through team intensives.

When combined with soft skills training, this effective strategy can be delivered in a management training curriculum. Coach skills training will serve to infuse *confidence* in your leaders. It will increase their performance and evoke a new leadership culture to drive greater results.

Coach skills training will help your executive leaders identify, equip, and empower more leaders *faster* than ever before. This is when growth in the development of your people moves forward with uncommon synergy and focus. Below are the ten training areas we cover—alongside soft skills training—during our two-year coach skills program.

1. Coach Training Essentials
2. Advanced Coaching Competencies
3. Coach Empowerment Tools
4. Theories, Frameworks, and Tools
5. ICF Mentor Coaching Skills Labs
6. Mentor Coaching Labs
7. Peer Coaching Labs
8. Coach Business Accelerators
9. Self-Directed Study Portfolio
10. Coach Performance Labs

3. On-Demand Training

Our third synergistic method is one of my favorites. On-Demand Training, ODT. Our Hybrid Coaching and Training approach consists of a combination of *self-directed* soft skills training and coach skills training streamed online.

Why is this one of my favorite training methods? It has to do with one word—*flexibility*. You're busy, and so are your leaders. You have time preferences throughout your day for learning, and so do they.

Personally, I enjoy self-directed learning from 5:30 AM – 7:30 AM. That's when I can give my best concentration to learning without interruptions. With ODT, time is no longer an obstacle.

"A key advantage of on-demand training is that it allows executives to fit their learning around their busy schedules, enabling them to acquire the knowledge and skills they need to perform better in their roles without disrupting their work and personal lives." Harvard Business Review, March 2020.[33]

Your leaders can watch these training videos and study at their own pace and time that works with their schedules. Most videos are 10-15 minutes in length and easily scheduled throughout the day.

---

[33] "The Benefits of On-Demand Learning for Executives," Harvard Business Review, March 2020.

4. Executive Coaching

Our fourth and final synergistic method—executive coaching—is one that simultaneously *accelerates* the execution and implementation of the HCCT program. Executive coaching connects the dots and delivers *sustainable* results for your leaders.

Ken Blanchard reminds us of the *powerful* impact of coaching on the lives of busy professionals. Coaching evokes new skills, increased behavioral knowledge, valuable experiences, goal orientation, self-reliance, increased responsibility, more productivity, better commitments, and higher levels of satisfaction.[34]

Executive coaching is about walking with you and your leaders through the process of discovery, options, and action. It evokes new awareness while creating effective plans to move you and your leaders from where you are to where you want to be.

In-person coaching is effective, but more studies reveal the exceptional results of online executive coaching. A significant amount of executive coaching has *shifted* to online platforms. This trend will continue to increase, especially in corporate environments.

---

[34] Ken Blanchard, "Managing Coaching for Results and ROI," (Escondido: The Ken Blanchard Companies, 2021), page 4.
https://resources.kenblanchard.com/whitepapers/managing-coaching-for-results-and-roi.

Distanced-based coaching—although perceived as negative for some regarding personalization and engagement—is a *more* favorable factor in the coaching process than a less favorable one. The benefits of in-person coaching are numerous indeed, but let's not discount the online benefits too quickly. There's no "one-size-fits-all" to coaching.

The effectiveness of executive coaching is not measured by the modality of coaching but rather by the effectiveness in helping my clients move forward along their journey.

Online coaching provides clients with the *flexibility* to work at their desired pace—and at their desired location—while allowing automatic reminders, emails, and tasks to help them follow on-demand training at a reasonable pace.[35]

Isn't this what you and your leaders want when it comes to key qualities of your professional development? Of course, it is. Empowering leaders to learn at their pace—and when convenient—communicates an extraordinary degree of trust *and* confidence.

In a most interesting research study, participants were asked what would be important to them regarding the process variables of in-person coaching, telephone coaching, and virtual coaching.

---

[35] Jeremy Sutton, "How Online Interventions Are Changing Coaching Forever," PositivePsychology.com, November 25, 2021, Accessed December 21, 2021, https://positivepsychology.com/online-coaching/.

Although initially skeptical about virtual coaching, participants experienced *increased* positivity scores once the virtual coaching sessions started. Surely, some of these participants were surprised by their positive results.

This research supports our original theory. Once people begin to experience online coaching, they will find numerous benefits and thoroughly enjoy the overall experience.[36]

The time for action has arrived.

The time to increase your professional effectiveness is now.

Are you ready to increase your performance—and the performance of your leaders and teams—with Hybrid Coaching and Training?

On your mark, get set, go!

---

[36] Harold Geissler, Melanie Hasenenbein, Stella Kanatouri, Robert Wegener, "E-Coaching: Conceptual and Empirical Findings of a Virtual Coaching Programme," International Journal of Evidence Based Coaching and Mentoring, Vol. 12, No. 2, (August 2014), Page 179, https://researchportal.coachfederation.org/MediaStream/PartialView?documentId=1889 (December 21, 2021).

The Coaching Advantage

Advantage #9

"Coaching can be an effective tool for developing new skills in leaders. Coaching can provide personalized guidance and feedback that is tailored to an individual's specific needs, which can be particularly beneficial for developing new skills. Leaders can develop skills through coaching, such as communication, decision-making, and emotional intelligence. **Coaching can be a valuable investment for individuals and organizations looking to improve their skills and performance.**"[37]

---

[37] Steve Cliffe, "Can Coaching Really Help Develop New Skills?" Forbes, August 12, 2020, https://www.forbes.com/sites/stevecliffe/2020/08/12/can-coaching-really-help-develop-new-skills/?sh=22073e4850d1.

Peter's Coaching Advantage

Peter's personality is highly contagious. He's humble, incredibly smart, and people-focused. His team was recovering from a difficult season. Morale was low, and several key players left his company without leaving someone qualified to fill their roles.

When our coaching session started, Peter was not discouraged by any means. On the contrary, he was *ready* to meet this new challenge with full force. Peter welcomed difficult challenges. And this challenge was, without question, complex.

Increase Your Performance with Hybrid Coaching and Training

How do you *simultaneously* equip executive leaders, managers, supervisors, and high-potential employees? What a good question, right? For starters, you think *outside* the box. This goes beyond training, but it absolutely includes training.

As we worked through where he wanted his company to land and the desired characteristics of his leaders and managers, Peter realized that it would require him to *leverage* a new methodology to impact the bottom line while developing his leaders faster than ever before.

1. **Soft Skills Training**
2. **Coach Skills Training**
3. **On-Demand Training**
4. **Executive Coaching**

Peter's desire to aggressively reduce the skills gap with his people motivated him to radically shift his thinking from absorbing a cost to making a wise investment. Your people are *worth* your investment.

Moreover, Peter not only wanted this training and coaching for his people, but he also wanted to be a key participant throughout the entire process.

He was so excited about the conversations I facilitated on his behalf that he actively participated in sketching out future sessions and what would be most relevant to his leaders.

Coaching and training will increase performance with your leaders and with their teams, but it must start with your commitment and investment to get better faster.

Peter's commitment to *modeling* what he expected from every leader and team member is a testament to what leadership looks like in the face of challenging times. Peter wasn't expecting miracles, but he was expecting forward progress. And that's exactly what he experienced with my help.

It is both humbling and rewarding to know that what you have to offer your clients is something that can change the entire *culture* of their business.

Hybrid Coaching and Training give your people the flexibility to learn at their own pace while challenging them to develop people-centric skills in a changing environment.

Questions for Reflection

1. How has the skills gap affected your performance and effectiveness as a leader?

2. How has it affected your leaders and their teams?

3. What have you learned in this chapter about the direct relationship coaching has on individual and team performance?

4. How much time, energy, and finances have you invested in developing your soft skills in the last year? What about for your key leaders and staff?

5. What led you to make the investment, or what factors held you back?

6. How would coach skills training give your leaders new tools to empower and equip more leaders faster?

7. How would on-demand training serve your leaders and their teams in practical ways?

8. What would you hope to accomplish by integrating executive coaching into the heartbeat of your monthly training and development strategy?

Chapter 10

Look Up

Discover Your Life's Purpose Outside of Yourself

Exposing Coaching Myths

Myth #11 – Coaching is only for business or career-related goals and nothing else.

The Real Story

Coaching has proven to have positive effects when pursuing goals for improving relationships, education, health, quality of life, conflicts, social media, finances, planning, initiative, competencies, experience, soft skills, church, or ministry involvement, and more.

Coaching positively impacts every area of life to help you get better faster.

People often ask me about the motivation behind what I do in my line of work. I mean, honestly, I love what I do. I invest my days serving others and helping people get better in the areas that matter most in their lives.

Before the choir of birds start singing next to my home office window in the early morning hours, I spend blocks of time praying, studying scripture, researching topics, and writing.

Shortly after, my day is filled with coaching, meetings, consulting, and training. I have the *privilege* of asking people what they really want to get out of life—their destination—and the *responsibility* to help them craft a personalized plan to get there.

Whether I'm on a ZOOM call with a business owner ready to sell their business or an ambitious executive ready to move up the corporate ladder, the work is very rewarding to the client and to me personally.

In the afternoons—and some evenings—you might find me Zooming with a married couple working through an extended relational plateau.

You may also find me sitting across the table with a business owner—as we drink a good cup of Cuban coffee—contemplating whether to sell their business and retire.

Honestly, I love helping people think deeply about these different challenges and what unique possibilities exist in each one. I walk them through a process to clarify what they want, evoke what's not being said, align with their values and goals, and focus on the next steps to move them forward.

My goal is to serve them with all my knowledge, experience, and skill as I generously give them my undivided attention.

God has blessed me with a loving wife and amazing children. I have a church family that is beyond gracious and supportive. By *God's* grace, I've been able to develop lasting friendships throughout the globe. My cup is indeed full.

The only way I've been able to publish more than twenty-five books, train thriving international businesses, and coach the finest leaders, has been through the encouragement of God's grace and the support of my family, my church, and my clients.

When given the opportunity to speak at conferences, lead training seminars, or facilitate executive retreats, I often take a moment to talk about my motivation for doing what I do every day.

I would like to finish this book by explaining the *source* of my increasing enthusiasm, motivation, and purpose for living. And in the process, I would like to help you consider *your* journey of faith and what's needed to move you forward in this key area of your life.

Look Up—Discover your purpose vertically

I remember the scene as if it were last night. I was a young boy looking up at the streetlight as darkness slowly conquered the day. As I looked up—and before my father whistled for me to run home—the question in my mind was simple yet profound.

It was the first existential question I remember asking myself. It had to do with discovering my purpose, understanding the meaning of life, and being able to plan and do what mattered in life.

I had loving parents, two younger brothers, one older sister, an aggressive rooster, and an ethnically diverse group of rambunctious friends. Life was great, but this question would not escape my mind.

"Isn't there more to this life than what I'm experiencing right now?"

It was a thunderous thought to reflect on and consider further. I was convinced that I needed to find the answer. But other questions surfaced.

Where do I start?

How will I know when I find my answer?

I was just a kid, not a philosopher or some great theologian. I was convinced that I was *not* the source of the answer I pursued. I would have to look *outside* myself—in a vertical direction—to find my answer.

"If any of you lacks wisdom, let him ask God, who gives generously to all without reproach, and it will be given him." – James 1:5

"Your word is a lamp to my feet and a light to my path." – Psalm 119:105

"And we know that for those who love God all things work together for good, for those who are called according to his purpose." – Romans 8:28

"For we are his workmanship, created in Christ Jesus for good works, which God prepared beforehand, that we should walk in them." – Ephesians 2:10

"As each has received a gift, use it to serve one another, as good stewards of God's varied grace: whoever speaks, as one who speaks oracles of God; whoever serves, as one who serves by the strength that God supplies—in order that in everything God may be glorified through Jesus Christ. To him belong glory and dominion forever and ever. Amen." – 1 Peter 4:10-11

A place to gather

Some time passed from the moment I asked the question to the day my mother decided the family would visit a local church in the neighborhood. It was a Spanish church with an American Pastor.

The entire worship experience was facilitated in Spanish. This was not my first language, but my ability to speak and understand what was being spoken was enough for me to get by.

Mom decided to make this local church our new church home. Although I captured most of what was being said, over time, I began to learn new things that stimulated my mind and heart.

There was a theme that resonated with my family during that time. Honestly, it was not something we had considered at all prior to attending this small church.

My parents were great parents. They worked hard to provide for our needs. However, spiritual life was not a part of our family life until my mother decided to take the first step and attend a worship service. Here's the theme.

Your spiritual relationship with God matters.

I must admit, this theme generated many questions. I was just a little dude trying to piece together what I was hearing and understanding. Little did I know that the answer to my original question would be discovered through the ministry of this new church family.

Be Honest: You're not as good as you think you are

As we continued attending this small church, I continued to grow in my understanding of God's Word—the Bible. Slowly but progressively, I started to feel *very* uncomfortable with some of my motives, words, and decisions in life.

I realized that I was very good at making *excuses* for my behavior. I was even better at getting my younger brothers in big trouble. Although young, I somehow mastered assigning blame to my brothers to avoid accepting responsibility for my words and actions.

Although I lived one way Monday through Saturday, I was *deeply* convicted every Sunday morning as I heard the Pastor explain the reality of our sinful nature—our fallen spiritual condition before a holy God.

Surely, he was not referring to me. After all, I was a little guy living in a big world. I was not responsible for my thoughts, words, or actions, right? I mean, we lived in a poor neighborhood. Crime encircled our community as drugs were distributed openly from popular street corners.

I was not that bad or that corrupt, right? I mean, the other guys were breaking into homes, stealing cars, and inflicting violence on others. But not me.

I was a *good* kid. I got into trouble at home and at school, but these were *mistakes*, immature errors, and unwise choices. But when I continued to hear the preaching of God's Word, the reality of my fallen nature—if I was honest—could *not* be hidden.

"As it is written: 'None is righteous, no, not one; no one understands; no one seeks for God. All have turned aside; together they have become worthless; no one does good, not even one."
– Romans 3:10-12

"For all have sinned and fall short of the glory of God." – Romans 3:23

"Therefore, just as sin came into the world through one man, and death through sin, and so death spread to all men because all sinned."
– Romans 5:12

"So whoever knows the right thing to do and fails to do it, for him it is sin."
– James 4:17

"We have all become like one who is unclean, and all our righteous deeds are like a polluted garment. We all fade like a leaf, and our iniquities, like the wind, take us away." – Isaiah 64:6

"And just as it is appointed for man to die once, and after that comes judgment." – Hebrews 9:27

Get Low: Humility is the catalyst to spiritual life

It's not until we humble ourselves—get low—before God that we begin to understand the *reality* of our fallen, sinful nature and the judgment to come. When I realized that God would *judge* my sin according to His Word, I humbled myself.

> **If you truly desire a spiritual breakthrough, you first must embrace the posture of humility in response to the reality of sin's presence in your life.**

Getting off on the wrong exit, not reviewing your presentation before meeting your client, or ordering something you're allergic to because you neglected to read the small print on the menu is an *unintended* error or a mistake, but it's not in the *sin* category.

Cheating on your taxes, manipulating reports, lying to your spouse, mistreating people, doing what you know is wrong, or not doing what you know is right are all in a different category altogether.

These are *not* unintended actions, innocent errors, or mistakes—these are *sins*. They directly violate God's Word, His standard for righteousness.

I may not have manipulated quarterly reports or lied to the IRS when I was a kid, but I certainly practiced things I knew were not right. There was a serious lack of congruence between what I heard on Sundays and what I practiced during the week. And every sin requires you to *repent* to be *forgiven*.

When Jesus started His ministry, He began with a brief but specific command.

"From that time Jesus began to preach, saying, 'Repent, for the kingdom of heaven is at hand.'" Matthew 4:17

It all started with a command to *"repent."* To *repent* means to dramatically *change* your *mind*—the way you think—leading to a change of *direction* in your life. It means you deliberately *exchange* your way of thinking for God's way of thinking.

This is not a casual activity or some passive approach to change. It requires deep humility. Repentance is *highly* intentional. And when you repent, change is *visible*. People can see it, and you can see it as well.

What I realized at a young age—although I believed that I was a good kid—was that I was seriously *out* of alignment with God's standard, the truth of God's Word. I had to be honest with God and assess my life according to His ways, His truth, and instruction, not mine.

You see, God wants you to evaluate *every* area of your life and measure it through His Word. And when you discover misalignment, repent—immediately *change* your thinking—confess your sins and radically change your direction.

What about you? Have you allowed God to radically *change* your way of thinking to *align* with His holy Word? Have you allowed God to *change* the direction of your life? If not, what's stopping you?

"Whoever conceals his transgressions will not prosper, but he who confesses and forsakes them will obtain mercy."
– Proverbs 28:13

"For the Father judges no one, but has given all judgment to the Son, that all may honor the Son, just as they honor the Father. Whoever does not honor the Son does not honor the Father who sent him. Truly, truly, I say to you, whoever hears my word and believes him who sent me has eternal life. He does not come into judgment, but has passed from death to life." – John 5:22-24

"Seek the Lord while he may be found; call upon him while he is near; let the wicked forsake his way, and the unrighteous man his thoughts; let him return to the Lord, that he may have compassion on him, and to our God, for he will abundantly pardon."
– Isaiah 55:6-7

And Peter said to them, "Repent and be baptized every one of you in the name of Jesus Christ for the forgiveness of your sins, and you will receive the gift of the Holy Spirit." – Acts 2:38

Be Real: Confess your sins

As I mentioned earlier, I was very skillful in manipulating others to get what I wanted. I steadily developed the skills of a charlatan without even understanding what that word meant. I must admit, it was a challenge, and it was enjoyable.

But it was not a pleasant feeling when it became clear that I was a *sinner* and had broken God's commandments. My personal enjoyment was not entertaining to God. God takes no pleasure in any form of deception.

To make matters worse, when I understood that I would be judged for my sins with perfect justice, things got real very fast. I was like Houdini, escaping from my personal responsibility for my words and actions. But when the curtain of God's Word was lowered and exposed my true self, the *guilt* of my sin was overwhelming.

I could easily deceive others, but I could never deceive God. I could lie with a smile, but God always sees and knows the truth. I could hide my true motives from others with a serious poker face, but God could see clearly through my expressions.

I realized that God sees—with divine clarity—my most *intimate* thoughts and the *true* motivation of my heart. He knows what directs what I think, what I say, and what I do. God knows *all* information about me. Honestly, that terrified me.

There was nowhere to run and nowhere to hide. God sees it all, even the things I don't want him to see. As I continued learning, three realities remained with me throughout the years.

God is omnipresent
He is always everywhere.
When you suffer loss, God is there.
When you celebrate a win, God is there. When you walk around the neighborhood, God is there.

God omniscient
He knows all things.
God has complete knowledge of time, space, and matter. There is nothing outside of God's knowledge. God is not surprised by anything. He has perfect knowledge of the past, present, and future.

God is omnipotent
He has all power and authority. God is more powerful than anything seen or unseen, created or produced, angelic or demonic. God has absolute power. He rules over all things. He keeps all things working according to His divine purposes.

"If we confess our sins, he is faithful and just to forgive us our sins and to cleanse us from all unrighteousness. If we say we have not sinned, we make him a liar, and his word is not in us."
– 1 John 1:9-10

"I acknowledged my sin to you, and I did not cover my iniquity; I said, 'I will confess my transgressions to the Lord,' and you forgave the iniquity of my sin." – Psalm 32:5.

"Because, if you confess with your mouth that Jesus is Lord and believe in your heart that God raised him from the dead, you will be saved. For with the heart one believes and is justified, and with the mouth one confesses and is saved." – Romans 10:9-10

"We have sinned and done wrong and acted wickedly and rebelled, turning aside from your commandments and rules." – Daniel 9:5

"Repent and be baptized every one of you in the name of Jesus Christ for the forgiveness of your sins, and you will receive the gift of the Holy Spirit."
– Acts 2:38

Be Hopeful: God provided the way for you to know Him

One Sunday after another—after much thought and deeper reflection—not only did my sin become evident, but so did the solution to my sin problem.

My sin was certainly the problem, but I was *not* the solution—Jesus was and is the *solution* to my sin—what separates me from a holy God. He is the God-ordained *way* to remove all my sins and have direct access to God.

Jesus is the way of God. He's the answer to your sin problem and the way to God.

One of the most well-known scripture passages tends to appear on billboards, football games, and countless printed materials. It was the scripture that provided me with *spiritual clarity*. Here is the first and second part of this key verse for context.

> "For God so loved the world, that he gave his only Son, that whoever believes in him should not perish but have eternal life. For God did not send his Son into the world to condemn the world, but in order that the world might be saved through him. Whoever believes in him is not condemned, but whoever does not believe is condemned already, because he has not believed in the name of the only Son of God."
> – John 3:16-18

We've established the reality of God's judgment because of sin's presence in our lives. But notice the reason for Jesus—the Son of God—coming to earth in the first place. He came to *save* those who *believed* in His name and give them eternal life. But wait, there's more.

Jesus is God's ONLY solution to your sin problem.

God gave His only son as the substitutionary sacrifice to *pay* the penalty for your sins. Jesus—The Lamb of God—paid for your sins once and for all as He shed His blood on the cross at Calvary. Jesus simultaneously *removed* sin's condemnation and *gave* you direct access to God the Father.

> "There is therefore now no condemnation for those who are in Christ Jesus. For the law of the Spirit of life has set you free in Christ Jesus from the law of sin and death." – Romans 8:1-2

> "For Christ also suffered once for sins, the righteous for the unrighteous, that he might bring us to God, being put to death in the flesh but made alive in the spirit." – 1 Peter 3:18

Jesus died on the cross for *your* sins. He was buried in a tomb and rose from the dead three days later. And what's the good news?

You can now live with great hope—and know God personally—when you **believe** in Jesus and **repent** of your sins.

"Therefore, since we have been justified by faith, we have peace with God through our Lord Jesus Christ."
– Romans 5:1

"For the wages of sin is death, but the free gift of God is eternal life in Christ Jesus our Lord." – Romans 6:23

"But to all who did receive him, who believed in his name, he gave the right to become children of God."
– John 1:12

Jesus said to him, "I am the way, and the truth, and the life. No one comes to the Father except through me." – John 14:6

"Because, if you confess with your mouth that Jesus is Lord and believe in your heart that God raised him from the dead, you will be saved. For with the heart one believes and is justified, and with the mouth one confesses and is saved."
– Romans 10:9-10

Believe: You connect with God through faith

So, when I finally connected the dots between my sin and God's provision for my sin—through the death, burial, and resurrection of Jesus—my heart responded in faith. I believed what God had said. Faith means you fully *believe* God, *trust* Him, and *follow* His Word.

I understood that you connect with God through *faith* by believing in Jesus' finished work on the cross and confessing your sins directly to Him through prayer. It was not about me. It was all about *Jesus* and what He did for me and for those who believe in His name.

My good deeds would always *miss* the mark.
My character would suffer loss and *fail*.
My intelligence would always be *insufficient*.
My motives would not always be *pure*.
My thoughts would not always be *holy*.
My words would eventually *hurt* others again.
My actions would not always be *good*.
My resources would never *solve* my issue.
My "good works" would never *replace* my past.
My dedication would never be *perfect*.
My money would be *inadequate* to pay for my sins.
My worship would not always be *vertical*.
My prayers would not always be *sincere*.

But God already knew these things. And still, God extended *grace*—unmerited favor—by sending Jesus to redeem us from our sins. Jesus did for us what we could *never* do for ourselves. And the thought of this is humbling and overwhelming.

"For by grace you have been saved through faith. And this is not your own doing; it is the gift of God, not a result of works, so that no one may boast. For we are his workmanship, created in Christ Jesus for good works, which God prepared beforehand, that we should walk in them."
– Ephesians 2:8-10

After listening to many sermons and conducting an *honest* assessment of my spiritual inventory, it was time for me to be real and get down to business, spiritually speaking, of course. I knew what my next step needed to be. It's simple: believe, confess, and receive.

Believe

When Jesus came on the scene, here's the first thing he said, "The time is fulfilled, and the kingdom of God is at hand; repent and believe in the gospel" (Mark 1:15).

Becoming a Christian means to believe in *Jesus*—his perfect life, death, burial, and resurrection (Romans 10:9).

Do you believe in Jesus Christ? If you do, tell him: "Lord Jesus, I believe that you are the Son of God. I believe in your sinless life and perfect obedience to the Father. I believe in your death on the cross, your burial, and your resurrection. And today, Lord, I rely on you as my Savior and Lord."

Confess

To confess means to *agree* with God about your sin. Your sin is enough to condemn you to an eternity in hell. You must come to terms with your utter hopelessness against sin apart from God's grace and mercy through Jesus Christ.

Are you ready to change from darkness to light, worldliness to godliness, sin to repentance?

If you're ready, tell him: "Lord Jesus, today I turn away from my sin and turn to you. I know that I have sinned against you and broken your commandments. I am fully responsible for my sins. I know that I have wronged you, Lord, through my sinfulness. I am deeply sorry for my sin. Please cleanse my heart and forgive me for all my sins. And thank you for offering Jesus as the wrath-bearing substitute for sinners like me! Help me, Lord, to follow your Word and never look back."

> "If you confess with your mouth the Lord Jesus and believe in your heart that God has raised Him from the dead, you will be saved."
> – Romans 10:9

Receive

Accept what God has graciously provided—His Son—for your eternal redemption. God has given you an indescribable gift, but He won't force it upon you. As one author said, "God loved, God gave, we believe, and we receive."

What do you do when someone you love gives you a gift? You reach out your hands and *receive* it gladly. Through a prayer of faith, tell God that you gladly receive the gift of life through Jesus Christ.

> "But as many as received Him, to them He gave the right to become children of God, to those who believe in His name." – John 1:12

Believe   Confess   Receive

Reach Up: You were designed for a spiritual relationship

I must admit, once I prayed to start following Jesus, not everything changed overnight. Yes, I was walking with Jesus—praying, reading scripture, attending church, and participating in communion. I experienced progressive, measurable *change*.

However, my spiritual growth did not launch in consistent rocket-like propulsion to the moon. At the start, it was back and forth, up and down, slow and steady. And from my experience, that's how most of us begin to discover our faith.

During this process of discovery, I realized that God's plan for my life was the *best* plan for me to follow. And if I followed God with all my heart, mind, soul, and strength, my life would be marked with increasing joy. That was the life that I desired.

> Jesus said, "The thief comes only to steal and kill and destroy. I came that they may have life and have it abundantly." – John 10:10

There was another component for me to learn. God created us for a *higher* purpose. Life was not about me, myself, or I. Life wasn't about getting what I wanted or getting ahead of others by any means necessary. It's about something far greater.

You were designed to love God and love others as you serve God's purposes and serve others.

You were designed for more than you can imagine. And by now, you've already noticed the surprising thread to experience the abundant life that Jesus promised. It's *relational*. God designed for you to experience a thriving spiritual relationship.

All God wants to do in and through your life flows from a spiritual relationship with Jesus.

This can be challenging to fully understand at first glance. But think about it. The reason God sent His Son to die on the cross for your sins was to establish a *direct* relationship with you—and those who would believe in Jesus.

Jesus used the metaphor of a vineyard to *illustrate* the importance of the spiritual relationship He desires with His disciples.

> "Abide in me, and I in you. As the branch cannot bear fruit by itself, unless it abides in the vine, neither can you, unless you abide in me. I am the vine; you are the branches. Whoever abides in me and I in him, he it is that bears much fruit, for apart from me you can do nothing." – John 15:4-5

God takes care of the vineyard. Jesus is the vine, and believers are His branches. The point Jesus makes is clear. The life and fruitfulness of your spiritual relationship are *sourced* in the vine—Jesus. Without this *continuous* connection, there is *nothing* spiritually productive that you can do without Him.

Start Working: Do the good God prepared for you to do

Once your spiritual relationship with Jesus begins, making time to explore what God wants you to *focus* your life on and *practice* is the next step.

God has a good plan for your life. This plan will not fall from heaven on your lap. It takes work. You must be intentional about understanding God's plan and committed to following wherever it leads you.

> "For we are his workmanship, created in Christ Jesus for good works, which God prepared beforehand, that we should walk in them."
> – Ephesians 2:8-10

When the Apostle Paul writes to the believers in Ephesus, he's not talking about *"good works"* in the sense of doing random acts of kindness. Paul has something more strategic and deliberate in mind.

You can help an elderly person cross the street, help a kid work through a math problem, or serve by picking up broken glass when the waiter's hand accidentally slips at the restaurant and drops your glass of water. These are all good things, and you should do good to serve people in these areas.

But we're referring to a much different focal point. In these three examples, you're helping the person. They are the focus of your service, and you are the only one getting the credit for helping and serving their needs.

Again, nothing bad here, but there's something *better* to strive for in your service to others.

When we talk about "good works" from a spiritual perspective, we're deliberately giving credit to Jesus as we help, meet needs, solve problems, and serve others.

This is the starting point of what we mean by doing *"good works"* in your walk of faith. The basis for serving others is deeply *rooted* in your abiding relationship with Christ (John 15:1-11). When you start serving others out of the *overflow* of your spiritual relationship, God can do great things through your life. This now becomes the primary source of your motivation.

Your primary motivation is no longer exclusively to help and serve others, although that's important. It's so much more than that.

In Christ, your motivation for serving and helping, giving, and sharing is so that others may look up—and see the love of Jesus— through your life. That's what "good works" are all about.

And as others experience God's love, mercy, and grace through *your* life, the hope is that they will come to *know* the Savior—Jesus Christ—and experience the abundant life that Jesus promised today and the hope of eternal life for their future.

Leverage Everything: Use all that you have for God's glory

As I matured in my faith, I began to understand an important principle—everything I have belongs to God. I don't own anything—God does. I serve as a *manager*—a steward—of God's resources. My purpose in life increases in clarity when I think and live like a manager, *not* an owner.

All that I have is sourced in God. Time, energy, talents, focus, health, experiences, education, relationships, finances, and other resources should be maximized to serve God's purposes.

Some may disagree or feel restricted by this statement above. For me, it was quite the opposite effect. Discovering that God was the source of all things in my life was enthusiastically *liberating*.

It was no longer about *getting* more things from life for yourself but *giving* more of what God gave you to others. It meant becoming a tool in God's hands, being ready to serve others whenever He opened the door to do so.

It was coming to the realization that when my life is *aligned* with God's Word—God's will and purpose for my life—I will be successful in whatever I set out to do. When it's not aligned, I won't.

Get Aligned: Be spiritually responsible for what matters

This section is borrowed from the introduction to one of my earlier books, *Aligned*. You can find the book on Amazon.com.

I remember the meeting like it was yesterday. I was hired by an international automotive company, along with my training partners, to help project managers *improve* their communication skills as they moved from one new project to another.

These exceptional engineers had worked with the company for a very long time.

But after countless video calls, phone meetings, and emails among team members, communication had started *declining* and fast. And after a short period of time, deadlines were *missed,* and costs started to *increase*. Prior to our engagement, those that should have accepted responsibility for delivering on their commitments were not doing so.

At the heart of their issue was an *unwillingness* to clearly define:

"*Who* is responsible?"

"*What* are they responsible for?" and

"*By when?*"—the due date for each commitment.

You may be asking at this point, "What do challenges within the automotive industry have to do with me being *aligned* with God?"

You have spiritual responsibilities given to you by God to understand, accept, and practice regularly.

As with my friends in the automotive industry, many believers today *lack* spiritual clarity and alignment when defining their spiritual responsibilities before God.

Why is this so important?

If you don't know what you're spiritually responsible for, you *won't* align your ways with God's ways. However, you remain *accountable* to fulfill your responsibilities before God. Consider the following questions as they relate to your life:

Is your life *aligned* with God's eternal purposes?

What are you spiritually responsible for?

Who are you spiritually responsible for?

What is the *purpose* of your life from God's perspective?

What *relationships* require more time, attention, and care?

What *resources* are you expected to *maximize* for God's purposes?

How can you maximize your *health* to honor God?

These questions lead us to explore the five areas of our framework for aligning our lives with God's purposes. By clearly understanding what you're responsible for from God's perspective, you can adjust and realign your life to follow God's ways with greater clarity.

I would like for you to filter each area of our framework through the lens of one transformational principle—seek *first* God's kingdom (Matthew 6:33). God is *first*.

This is the order of divine blessing for *your* life and every believer. As you accept this challenge, you will experience God's *power, provision, direction,* and *protection* in more ways than you can imagine.

> Jesus said, "But seek first the kingdom of God and his righteousness, and all these things will be added to you." – Matthew 6:33

Let's summarize each essential area of our framework. This framework will provide you with a biblical model to live your life in such a way that God is pleased. How can you do this?

By living by *faith* in God through Jesus Christ as you follow God first and His will for your life in all things (Hebrews 11:6).

My Spiritual Life

Is God *first* in your *spiritual life*? Do you spend time with God *before* your day starts moving? Your daily relationship with Christ is your *most* important priority. Your inner life matters.

The quality of your spiritual relationship with Christ must be nurtured and cultivated (John 15:1-11). To thrive spiritually, you need increasing measures of quantity and quality in your relationship with Christ.

Jesus came to *change* you from darkness to light. He wants you to *experience* Him daily through an abiding relationship. Practicing the presence of Jesus is powerful. It's what you need every day to thrive spiritually.

As you further develop your spiritual habits, your prayer life will change, and so will your ability to connect people to Jesus.

Your spiritual life overflows into every other area of your life. It will determine how you live out your purpose as a believer. It drives how you invest in relationships to point people to Christ. It directly affects the way you manage your resources. And finally, your spiritual life *moves* you to act.

My Purpose

Is God *first* in your personal mission and *purpose* for living? Do your values reflect God's values? Life is *not* about you. You are not the center—God *is*. You are not in charge—God *is*.

Your life in Christ has a specific purpose—to glorify God.

How do you do that?

You love God, and you love people.
You serve God, and you serve people.
You work for God, and you work with people.
Your life was designed to glorify God by directing, working, serving, and maximizing God's creation for God's kingdom purposes.

My Relationships

Is God *first* in your *relationships*? Relationships matter to God, and they should matter to you. God wants you to be *Christlike* at school, with people at work, among friends, and with those in your family.

He wants you to model the character of Christ, even with those who regularly test your patience or even drive you crazy at times.

God's desire is for you to develop rich spiritual friendships with His people and genuine friendships with those who don't know Christ.

His desire is for you to *coach* and *train* believers in their spiritual growth as you continue learning from Christ and from His people.

My Resources

Is God *first* in the way you maximize His resources? Do you consistently *prioritize* His kingdom and apply His principles in the way you manage and maximize what He's provided?

God doesn't expect you to manage or maximize what you don't have. But you will give an account of the resources God gave you to expand for His glory.

Is God *first* in the way you maximize your *time*? Your time on this earth is *limited*. God has given you a measure of time to use for His eternal purposes.

You can waste this limited resource, or you can maximize it for His kingdom purposes. You can't buy more time or extend your day beyond 24 hours.

You must make the most of every day to do your best with the time that you have.

Is God *first* in the way you maximize your *talents*? Are you making the most of your uniqueness, personality, preferences, and special abilities? There's no one else on earth like you. This is *not* accidental.

Is God *first* as you seek to develop your *skills*? Are you intentionally using your education, training, and experiences to *serve* God's kingdom purposes? God has given you the capacity to *thrive*. Make sure you're maximizing what He's given you.

The Lord formed you in a special way to fulfill His eternal purposes. Seek to be the person *God* designed you to be so that others can clearly see salt and light expressed through your life every day.

Is God *first* in the way you manage and maximize your treasures? There is no greater *indicator* of what's leading your heart at this very moment than *where* you've *placed* your treasure. Your heart *always* follows where you *place* your treasure.

God wants you to give, save, invest, and spend in ways that *honor* Him. But as we've mentioned earlier, He needs to be *first* in every area, including your finances and material possessions.

My Health

Is God *first* in the way you care for your *health*? Are you consistent in maximizing this area of your life? Would the people around you agree or disagree with your answer?

Do you really believe that your body is the *temple* of the Holy Spirit (1 Corinthians 6:19-20)?

Living a disciplined life—in how you manage your health and other areas—maximizes your impact for God's purposes.

It doesn't honor God at all when you get *lazy* in this area. You need to establish *sustainable* exercise, nutrition, rest, and sleep habits in your schedule. You need to *replenish* your mind and soul through planned times of silence and solitude.

If you consistently neglect to manage and care for your body, you will experience a physical, emotional, and/or mental health crisis in the future.

Here's the good news: You can do life better, and you don't have to do it alone. With coaching, you have a *distinct* advantage to get better—in each of these areas and others—faster. Let's look closer at this special advantage in our conclusion.

The Coaching Advantage

Advantage #10

"Coaching can help individuals identify and pursue their purpose. Understanding one's purpose can provide clarity, motivation, and a sense of fulfillment, which can translate into improved performance in both personal and professional life. Leaders who have discovered their purpose have made significant contributions in their fields. **Coaching can help individuals clarify their values, strengths, and goals and develop a plan to align these with their purpose.**"[38]

---

[38] Sallie Krawcheck, "What Is Your Life's Purpose? Why You Need to Find It to Be a More Effective Leader," Fortune, November 30, 2020, https://fortune.com/2020/11/30/life-purpose-effective-leader-career-success/.

Questions for Reflection

1. What thoughts come to mind as you reflect deeper on your life's *purpose* from a spiritual perspective?

2. What was helpful as we reviewed the importance of *vertically* discovering your life's purpose, looking beyond yourself, and starting with God to find your answer?

3. How would you explain to someone else what it means to be honest with God?

4. As humility serves as the catalyst to your spiritual life, what thoughts surfaced when you read, "If you truly desire a spiritual breakthrough, you first must embrace the posture of humility in response to the reality of sin's presence in your life."

5. Have you taken the step to believe, confess, and receive *Jesus* as Savior? If not, what's holding you back?

6. Which of these spiritual responsibilities are your *weakest* and require more attention: My Spiritual Life, My Purpose, My Relationships, My Resources, or My Health?

7. Which of the spiritual responsibilities listed is your *strongest*?

Conclusion

Your Coaching Advantage

Move Forward   Lead Confidently   Accelerate Performance

The adventure and the opportunity of maximizing key areas of your life is worth your investment of time, energy, finances, and focus. The time to get better, faster, is *now*.

As you commit to your personal growth in key areas of your life—in combination with coaching—you will gain a more comprehensive and biblical perspective on how God wants to bless others through *your* life. It begins as you seek God's will *first* in each of these areas. That's the secret sauce!

What is *your* coaching advantage?

By now, I think you've figured it out. Coaching helps you to *focus* on what matters most in your life. It *removes* the clutter and sets aside distractions that keep you busy but are ineffective.

Coaching helps you *create* a path from where you are to where you want to be in life. It *defines* what really matters. Coaching *clarifies* what remains unclear and *asks* penetrating questions that stir your soul and challenge your mind.

Coaching keeps you *accountable* for the commitments you make. Without any emotional attachment, coaching provides you with *honest* observations and feedback. It *calls* you out when you make excuses and acknowledges your effort when you're making progress.

It helps you to establish *agreements* that are realistic but challenging, thought-provoking but achievable, and, at times, ambitious but truly inspirational.

Coaching serves to evoke new perspectives about your situation while giving you full ownership to lead the way forward. The coach is not in charge of your life—you are. The coach is not the one acting on your commitments—you are. The coach is present to guide you in the process of moving what matters most in your life forward.

Coaching is you-focused and *action*-driven. It is purposeful and deliberate. It is both exciting and convicting for the soul to experience.

No other professional relationship can impact your life like coaching can. Although coaching has taken off in the business world, it is having a *profound* effect on the lives of educational leaders, students, nonprofit executives, managers, and many others.

You don't "need" to move forward in your life.

You don't "need" to lead yourself better or lead others better.

You don't "need" to realize your dreams.

The question is, "Do you want to do these things?"

Do you want to lead confidently and move forward in your life?

Do you want to lead yourself better and lead others better?

Do you want to accelerate your performance?

And if your answer is a decisive "Yes I do!" then make a commitment today to hire an expert coach and get started.

The Coaching Advantage

Everybody knows that coaching is needed in businesses, organizations, educational institutions, churches, other religious institutions, and the government, but not everybody is taking *advantage* of what transformative coaching has to offer.

What about *you*?

Are you maximizing what you have by gaining a *competitive* advantage in life through coaching? You regularly invest in professional training with other colleagues. You separate blocks of time on your calendar and commit to the training.

You clearly see the benefits of this investment, but what about coaching? What if I told you that training has *limitations*? I know that may sound rather strange coming from a professional soft skills trainer, but it's true.

I've trained some of the world's most respected professionals. These men and women are brilliant. They read continuously, devour audiobooks for breakfast, and stay current on new market trends.

Some of these leaders choose to invest in coaching *early* in their careers or prior to starting their new businesses.

For other leaders, coaching often begins where training ends. There's only so much information you can process and make relevant to your world today.

Coaching serves to *leverage* everything you've learned in education, training, and life—both personal and professional—to *maximize* its application for your next move forward.

This highly intentional focus to help leaders gain a *unique* advantage professionally and personally is, by far, the most exciting part of my work with business leaders and thriving executives.

Working with an experienced coach undoubtedly gives you a *clear* advantage in life. I know from experience. I meet with coaches regularly to get better faster. I don't pretend to have all the answers.

I *want* other coaches to challenge my thinking and draw out the very best in me so that I can continue making an impact in the lives of others. It's not the *only* method to grow, but it is certainly a *wise* approach to personal and professional growth.

I hope *The Coaching Advantage* has served as a source of encouragement to strengthen you professionally and personally. I hope it has served to challenge some of your perspectives and default approaches to challenges and obstacles.

I also hope that this book has given you a greater appreciation for *people*—especially those you love and lead every day—and the untapped capacity they possess for moving from good to great. Your coaching advantage is what *launches* the entire process of developing others.

You can only coach others effectively after you've experienced effective coaching for yourself.

Redeem the time you have left on this earth for something *greater* than yourself. Move forward, lead confidently, and accelerate your performance today!

About Marcel Sanchez

Marcel has been *enthusiastically* married to his wife Yami for over 31 years and has two adult children, Luke, and Savanah.

Marcel is a Certified Professional Coach and accredited through the International Coaching Federation, ICF. He graduated with a B. A. in Human Resources Management from Trinity International University and a Master of Arts in Organizational Management from the University of Phoenix. Additionally, he has completed many theological certifications, courses, and intensives.

Marcel has published over twenty-six books and training guides. He loves to think deeply about creating interactive courses to help people grow professionally, relationally, and spiritually.

Marcel is also a licensed and ordained Pastor and currently serves as the Executive Pastor at Global Church (www.GlobalChurch.me), a bilingual church in Miami, Florida. In his free time, Marcel enjoys spending time with family, writing, building courses, and helping people follow Jesus.

If you're ready to gain a unique advantage in life through professional coaching, contact Marcel directly.

Phone or Text: +1-786-554-0312

Email: ImagineCoachingAcademy@gmail.com

Move Forward   Lead Confidently
Accelerate Performance

References

1. *"What is Coaching?"* International Coaching Federation. ICF.org. Accessed December 21, 2021, https://coachingfederation.org/about.

2. Merriam-Webster.com Dictionary, s.v. "blind spot," accessed January 2, 2023, https://www.merriam-webster.com/dictionary/ blind%20spot.

3. "How to Identify and Remove Blind Spots in Your Business." Forbes, 24 Jan. 2023, www.forbes.com/sites/forbesbusinesscouncil/2019/01/12/how-to-identify-and-remove-blind-spots-in-your-business/?sh=6a54a16d7599

4. Gregersen, Hal B., and Emma-Sue Prince Van Oosten. The Leader's Guide to Corporate Culture: How to Manage the Eight Critical Elements of Organizational Life. John Wiley & Sons, 2018.

5. Dweck, Carol S. Mindset: The New Psychology of Success. Random House, 2006, p.35

6. Schreiner, William. "Coaching Executives to Success: A Review of Executive Coaching Research." Journal of Business and Psychology 36, no. 2 (2021): 255-278.

7. ICF Global Coaching Client Study https://www.ipeccoaching.com/hubfs/What%20is%20Coaching%20-%20iPEC%20Coach%20Training.pdf

8. https://www.american.edu/provost/ogps/executive-education/executive-coaching/roi-of-executive-coaching.cfm

9. https://www.forbes.com/sites/russalanprince/2018/10/08/why-business-coaching-is-booming/?sh=337b5df720ff

10. Anderson, Michael, and David Day. "Coaching executives for innovation: Insights from high-tech firms." Journal of Business Research 113 (2020): 348-357.

11. Ken Blanchard, "Managing Coaching for Results and ROI," (Escondido: The Ken Blanchard Companies, 2021), page 4. https://resources.kenblanchard.com/whitepapers/managing-coaching-for-results-and-roi.

12. Judith Jordan, Relational–cultural theory: The power of connection to transform our lives. The Journal of Humanistic Counseling, 56(3), (2017) 228-243. https://onlinelibrary.wiley.com/doi/abs/10.1002/johc.12055. (Accessed December 21, 2021).

13. What is Coaching? Everything You've Wanted to Know, (iPec Coaching) December 21, 2021, https://www.ipeccoaching.com/hubfs/What%20is%20Coaching%20-%20iPEC%20Coach%20Training.pdf

14. Andrea Kysely et al., "Expectations and Experiences of Couples Receiving Therapy Through Videoconferencing: A Qualitative Study.," Frontiers in Psychology 10 (2019): 2992, https://doi.org/10.3389/fpsyg.2019.02992. (Accessed December 21, 2021).

15. Geiger, Jenna. "The Benefits of Marriage Coaching for Business Leaders." Entrepreneur. January 27, 2021. https://www.entrepreneur.com/article/363078.

16. O'Shea, Donal. "The Impact of Executive Coaching on the Work-Life Balance of Business Leaders." Journal of Applied Psychology 105, no. 3 (2021): 245-257.

17. Whitmore, John. Coaching for Performance: Growing People, Performance, and Purpose. Nicholas Brealey Publishing, 2005.

18. Starling, Stephanie. "How Executive Coaching Can Help You Overcome Career Obstacles." Forbes. February 16, 2021. https://www.forbes.com/sites/stephanieburns/2021/02/16/how-executive-coaching-can-help-you-overcome-career-obstacles/?sh=215b06454e04.

19. "Evoke." Merriam-Webster.com Dictionary, Merriam-Webster, https://www.merriam-webster.com/dictionary/evoke. Accessed 20 Feb. 2023.

20. Dalton, Rachel. "How life coaching can help you develop a better life plan." Fast Company. January 11, 2021. https://www.fastcompany.com/90592305/how-life-coaching-can-help-you-develop-a-better-life-plan.

21. Pollak, Jolie. "How Coaching Can Help You Reach Goals That Seemed Unattainable." The New York Times. February 23, 2021. https://www.nytimes.com/2021/02/23/smarter-living/coaching-unattainable-goals.html.

22. International Coach Federation (ICF), ICF Global Coaching Client Study (Lexington, KY: International Coach Federation, 2009)

23. Richard J. Jones, Stephanie A. Woods, and Yves R. F. Guillaume, "The effectiveness of workplace coaching: A meta-analysis of learning and performance outcomes from coaching," Journal of Occupational and Organizational Psychology 88, no. 2 (2015)

24. Manchester Inc., "Building a coaching culture: Key strategies for embedding coaching skills and practices into your organization" (2001)

25. Khan, Muhammad Jahanzeb, and Sami Farooq. "The impact of coaching on employee performance: Evidence from the banking sector of Pakistan." International Journal of Training and Development 25, no. 1 (2021): 71-87.

26. American Management Association. "Coaching: A global study of successful practices." Accessed March 3, 2023. https://www.amanet.org/articles/coaching-a-global-study-of-successful-practices/.

27. Torch. "Leveraging Coaching and Mentoring to Create More Effective Leaders." Harvard Business Review, January 2023, accessed March 3, 2023, https://torch.io/wp-content/uploads/2023/01/Leveraging-Coaching-and-Mentoring-to-Create-More-Effective-Leaders_Torch_HBRAS.pdf.

28. Capranos, D., Magda, A. J. (2023). Closing the skills gap 2023: Employer perspectives on educating the post pandemic workforce. Maitland, FL: Wiley Inc.

29. Torch. "Leveraging Coaching and Mentoring to Create More Effective Leaders." Harvard Business Review, January 2023, accessed March 3, 2023, https://torch.io/wp-content/uploads/2023/01/Leveraging-Coaching-and-Mentoring-to-Create-More-Effective-Leaders_Torch_HBRAS.pdf.

30. "Soft Skills." Oxford Learner's Dictionaries. Accessed March 6, 2023. https://www.oxfordlearnersdictionaries.com/us/definition/english/soft-skills?q=soft+skills.

31. Torch. "Leveraging Coaching and Mentoring to Create More Effective Leaders." Harvard Business Review, January 2023, accessed March 3, 2023, https://torch.io/wp-content/uploads/2023/01/Leveraging-Coaching-and-Mentoring-to-Create-More-Effective-Leaders_Torch_HBRAS.pdf.

32. "What is Coaching?" International Coaching Federation, ICF.org, December 21, 2021, https://coachingfederation.org/about

33. Harvard Business Review. "The Benefits of On-Demand Learning for Executives." March 2020.

34. Ken Blanchard. "Managing Coaching for Results and ROI." (Escondido: The Ken Blanchard Companies, 2021). page 4. https://resources.kenblanchard.com/whitepapers/managing-coaching-for-results-and-roi.

35. Jeremy Sutton, "How Online Interventions Are Changing Coaching Forever," PositivePsychology.com, November 25, 2021, Accessed December 21, 2021, https://positivepsychology.com/online-coaching/.

36. Harold Geissler, Melanie Hasenenbein, Stella Kanatouri, Robert Wegener. "E-Coaching: Conceptual and Empirical Findings of a Virtual Coaching Programme." International Journal of Evidence Based Coaching and Mentoring. Vol. 12, No. 2, (August 2014), https://researchportal.coachfederation.org/MediaStream/PartialView?documentId=1889 (December 21, 2021).

37. Cliffe, Steve. "Can Coaching Really Help Develop New Skills?" Forbes. August 12, 2020. https://www.forbes.com/sites/stevecliffe/2020/08/12/can-coaching-really-help-develop-new-skills/?sh=22073e4850d1.

38. Krawcheck, Sallie. "What Is Your Life's Purpose? Why You Need to Find It to Be a More Effective Leader." Fortune, November 30, 2020. https://fortune.com/2020/11/30/life-purpose-effective-leader-career-success/.

Made in the USA
Columbia, SC
20 April 2023